THE LAST GANG IN TOWN

THE LAST GANG IN TOWN

The Epic Story of the Vancouver Police vs. the Clark Park Gang

Aaron Chapman

ARSENAL PULP PRESS
VANCOUVER

THE LAST GANG IN TOWN

SECOND PRINTING: 2016

ARSENAL PULP PRESS
Suite 202 – 211 East Georgia St.
Vancouver, BC V6A 1Z6
Canada
arsenalpulp.com

The publisher gratefully acknowledges the support of the Canada Council for the Arts and the British Columbia Arts Council for its publishing program, and the Government of Canada (through the Canada Book Fund) and the Government of British Columbia (through the Book Publishing Tax Credit Program) for its publishing activities.

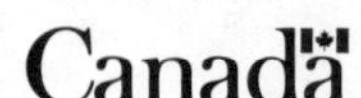

Canadä

Cover and text design by Oliver McPartlin
Edited by Susan Safyan
Cover image: City of Vancouver Archives, cropped version of map PD 2100.3

Printed and bound in Canada

Library and Archives Canada Cataloguing in Publication:
Chapman, Aaron, 1971–, author
The last gang in town : the epic story of the police vs the Clark Park gang / Aaron Chapman.

Issued in print and electronic formats.
ISBN 978-1-55152-671-3 (paperback).—ISBN 978-1-55152-672-0 (html)

1. Clark Park Gang. 2. Gangs—British Columbia—Vancouver—History—20th century. 3. Gang members—British Columbia—Vancouver—History—20th century. 4. Undercover operations—British Columbia—Vancouver—History—20th century. 5. Police shootings—British Columbia—Vancouver—History—20th century. 6. Vancouver (B.C.)—History—20th century. 7. Vancouver (B.C.)—Social conditions—20th century. I. Title.

HV6439.C32V2 2016 364.106′60971133 C2016-904927-2
C2016-904928-0

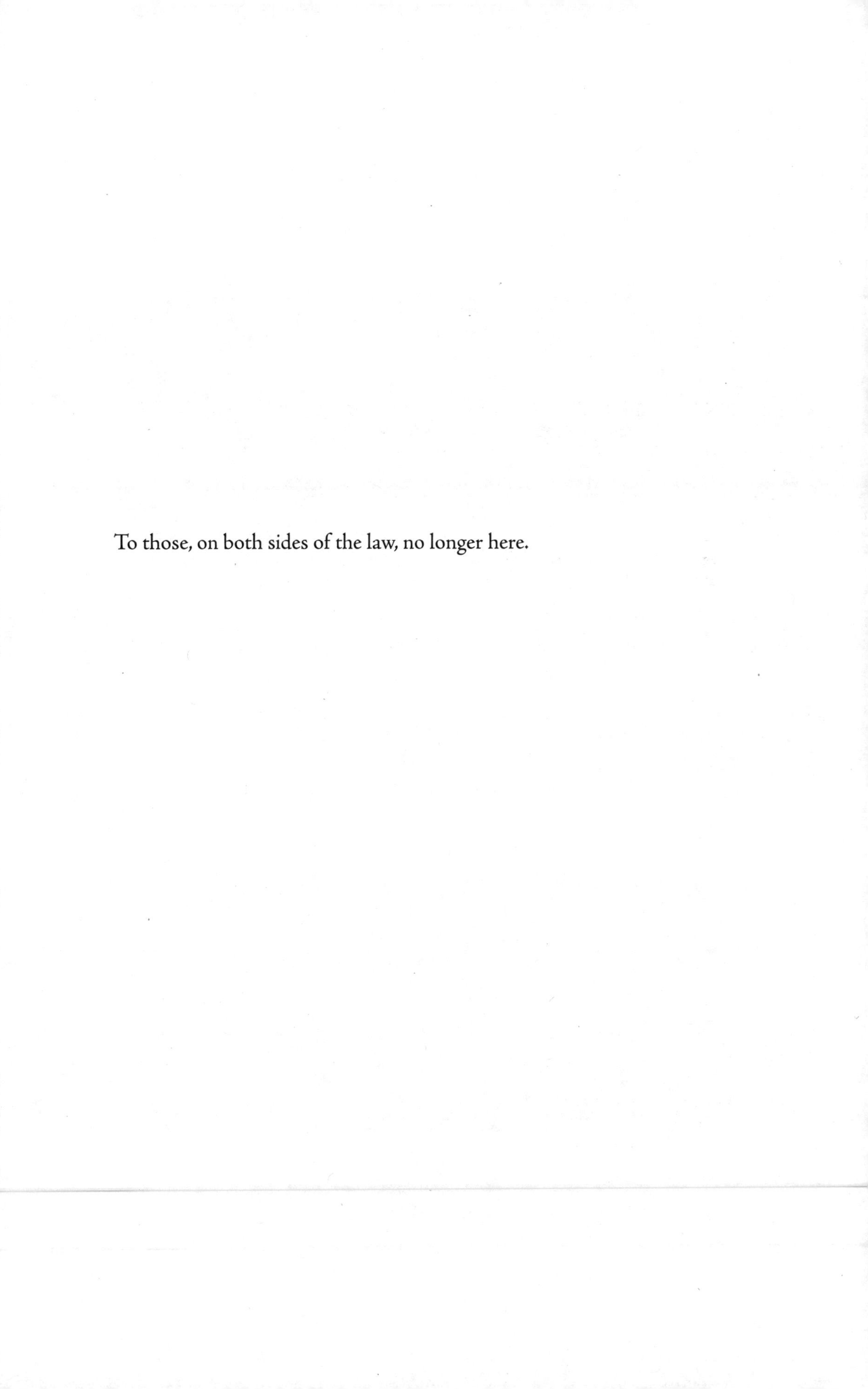

To those, on both sides of the law, no longer here.

CONTENTS

INTRODUCTION

The Clark Park gang. The worst of the worst. Hell-born, long-haired thugs from a generation of bastards raised on the hard streets in the East End of Vancouver. The brutal street gang erupted into violence everywhere they went, beating up everyone in sight. They'd arrive out of nowhere only to disappear back down into the dirty bowels of East Vancouver by the time police showed up—ready to put on knuckles, ready to fight, with a fist across your face, leaving you conscious just long enough to smell the sleeve of a faded red mack jacket that stinks of nicotine and rage.

The rev of an engine fed on leaded gasoline, the swing of a bike chain. A faceless bunch of troublemakers, delinquents, and goons, who'd catch you on the wrong side of town and, making good on a threat, sink a Dayton boot into your stomach with a laugh, only to roar like monster hellions back to Clark Park, their would-be headquarters and stomping ground, itself full of buried weapons and bad attitude.

They were always ready for anyone who dared cross them on their own turf. You'd leave bloodied, never to forget the experience. The Clark Parkers, ready to show up at anytime, anywhere, tonight ... In the criminal history of Vancouver, they remain notorious villains, yet still full of mystery.

These are just some of the stories, rumours, truths, and lies about the Clark Park gang that Vancouverites were confronted with, especially in the relatively innocent years of the 1970s when they were known as dangerous street thugs, a period before Vancouver gangs became more interested in the money and guns associated with the international drug trade.

It is one of the least-known episodes in Vancouver's criminal history, a time when street gangs, many associated with individual city parks, roamed the East End and in the process, attained a shadowy, mythical status that persists to this day.

And myth is a fitting term. Vancouver police and city prosecutors at the time only vaguely mentioned the gang amidst broad recriminations against the counterculture of the period. Television news didn't accurately report on them, and while newspaper reporters of the era may have name-dropped the Clark

Park gang from time to time, they never fully gained their trust enough to get an interview with members. Yet for a time, the Clark Park name was all over the city, and for decades the gang was presumed responsible for almost any assault, burglary, car theft, drug deal, or riot of the period.

Vancouver is a great deal different now than it was then. For one thing, the look of the city no longer changes markedly when you cross Main Street from west to east. While the dozen or so city blocks that make up the Downtown Eastside remain an area troubled by crime and open drug use, East Vancouver in general is no longer considered the tough working-class part of town or the wrong side of the tracks.

Now a new generation resides in East Vancouver, made up of university professors, dentists, lawyers, film technicians, website designers, or interior decorators who own expensive, refurbished, single-family homes that once belonged to tradesmen, warehousemen, sanitation workers, sheet-metal workers, and longshoremen. There are now multi-million dollar homes in East Van, just as there are in the tony Kerrisdale neighbourhood on the city's west side.

The iconic "East Van" cross that was once a popular subject for graffiti in the East End—to some, an emblem of community pride, to others, associated with area gangs—today stands prominently as a public installation by artist Ken Lum. And while back then a thug in a mack jacket might have greeted an outsider with a swinging baseball bat, now the white, LED-lit twenty-metre sign innocuously welcomes all who enter the neighbourhood. As time goes by, fewer and fewer people will remember East Vancouver's recent past or recognize the cross as the symbol of a "tough East Ender," and it seems almost certain that this archetype will seem less relevant as gentrification continues its march through this part of the city.

There are both police officers and former gang members who still simply don't wish to talk about the Clark Park gang in the early 1970s. Some constables who were integrally involved with the policing of the gang destroyed their personal notebooks upon retirement and continue to decline interviews. Others now feel comfortable enough to begin to recall this vivid time in their careers. As constable Brian Honeybourn told me, "I've never spoken of this in over forty years. I've never talked to the media. I've never really spoken about this with my own family until now." And some of those who were once a part of the Clark Park gang are no longer phantoms—they do exist—though their numbers are dwindling. They remember a Vancouver that doesn't exist but disappeared only a relatively short time ago.

Neither side has divulged their stories until now. In *The Last Gang in Town,* both sides tell two-fisted tales. Former gang members can tell you about the rumbles and fights that took place throughout East Vancouver as well as the laughs and tears they shared while incarcerated, whether in juvenile detention or in maximum-security Oakalla prison. The police, meanwhile, recall memories of the deafening noise being on the front lines of a riot squad and of being tasked with a mission that they had never before been asked to handle so covertly or so aggressively. Both sides have friends who are no longer alive, who never made it this far. And many are still connected by the sound of a gunshot that rang out in the middle of the night in Vancouver's Mount Pleasant area almost forty-five years ago, the echoes of which are still heard today.

Today the East Van Cross installation by artist Ken Lum at Clark Drive and Great Northern Way welcomes outsiders entering East Vancouver. It wasn't always that way. The symbol has roots in the area going back at least sixty years.
PHOTO: Michal Urbánek, 2016

ONE: DOWN AND OUT IN EAST VANCOUVER

Today, Vancouver's citizens discuss concerns over the cost of living and the problems of home affordability with the grave tones that other cities usually reserve for the topic of violent crime—which, according to most evening news reports, is now all but restricted to the suburbs. It wasn't always so. The 1986 World's Fair—Expo 86—is commonly cited as the event that changed Vancouver's small-town sensibility forever. But was it a change for the better? This is hotly debated; many residents nostalgically remember Expo favourably while others believe it destroyed the city's character. But the first significant signs of change in Vancouver took place considerably earlier than Expo, when Vancouver could be seen as two different and distinct cities.

More than fifty years ago, Vancouver started to undergo changes resulting from zoning bylaws, immigration, and industry that would begin to shape not only its size and density, but also the kind of policing issues it would face in the future. The city's downtown core and West End would undergo drastic change in the 1960s, thanks to new zoning bylaws that encouraged the development of 220 highrises and apartment buildings, creating a new city skyline where single-family, three-storey homes had stood before.[1]

The economy of British Columbia was still being driven by large lumber companies such as MacMillan Bloedel, and that industry coated the province in sawdust, even in downtown Vancouver, where log booms sat next to the wharves on False Creek. From the 1920s to the beginning of the 1960s, False Creek "rivalled Pittsburgh for smoke output."[2] But this was beginning to change. As Vancouver historian Bruce MacDonald notes: "In 1963 there were just three sawmills left in False Creek. The utilization of sawmill waste in BC's new pulp mills and the subsequent disappearance of smoking beehive burners greatly reduced the amount of smoke in the city's air and halted the

1 Bruce MacDonald, *Vancouver: A Visual History* (Vancouver, BC: Talonbooks, 1992), 55.
2 Michael Kluckner, *Vancouver: Between the Streets* (Vancouver, BC: Consolidated Merriment Ltd., 1981), 121.

number of foggy days compared to the 1940s."[3]

In the 1960s, some properties in the city sold for less than they had in 1912[4], but by the early 1970s new and old homeowners were becoming property speculators, and within just a few years a real estate boom doubled property values. However, while downtown and west side residents were experiencing a sense of growth and a promise of prosperity, East Vancouver was a different story. The east side neighbourhood of Strathcona was regarded as a blighted area. Even before the 1967 proposal to run a freeway through it, areas of East Vancouver were slated for demolition. Since the 1950s, banks would not lend money to area residents for home improvements. In general, East Vancouver was not often regarded as an attractive neighbourhood, especially in comparison to the west side of the city.

In fact, for much of Vancouver's history the west and east sides of Vancouver were seen as two very distinct parts of town. They differed in attitudes, occupations, cultural makeup, and political affiliations, with residents on the west side typically white-collar workers, and those on the east side mostly blue-collar and less prosperous.

While the East Van neighbourhood surrounding Commercial Drive is today regarded as a multicultural area, home to a broad array of eateries and cafés, and where a left-of-centre cool is seen in abundant supply on the sidewalks and in its stores, in the 1960s East Vancouver had none of this. Students, artists, musicians, and the counterculture were more often found in the west side neighbourhood of Kitsilano, near the University of British Columbia. East Van was yet to undergo the influx of Vietnamese and Latin American immigrants in the late 1970s and '80s that resulted in new ethnic businesses on Commercial Drive. In the early 1970s, the area was widely regarded as Vancouver's Little Italy.

There was plenty of colour and personality in the neighbourhood: On the street, the sounds of children taking accordion lessons in the back of barber shops could be heard mixed with the shouts of adults playing cards or doing a little wagering on the horse races at Exhibition Park. Women walking by themselves along Commercial Drive in the afternoons were used to being catcalled or whistled at. Some ignored it, but others fired back with vivid Italian

3 MacDonald, 55.
4 Ibid., 60.

swear words or hand gestures they'd learned even if they themselves weren't Italian. East Vancouver children learned to skate on Trout Lake back when the winter froze it over, and learned to swim there in the summer.

Many Commercial Drive businesses that Vancouverites would now consider venerable institutions didn't open until the 1970s, such as Joe's Café in 1974 (although Nick's Spaghetti House has been on the Drive since 1955). Other stores included Grippo Television Repair, Manitoba Hardware, Norman's Market, and Longo's Auto Shop, along with Monty's Pool Hall and Grandview Billiards (open since 1921, until it closed in the early 2000s, and today home to Falconetti's East Side Grill and The Cannibal Café)[5]. For a bite to eat, you could go to Wally's Burgers, but you could also find home-cooked burgers made by the old-timer off Victoria Drive who grilled them on his hibachi and sold them right off the front stoop of his apartment building.

Commercial Drive circa 1960s.
PHOTO: Walter E. Frost, City of Vancouver Archives, CVA 447-310

Down at the corner of Princess and Hastings streets was Curly's Tattoos, run by the wheelchair-bound Curly Allen himself (real name John W. Weatherhead). Although paralyzed on his left side, he inked thousands of tattoos in East Vancouver for generations, always with an ever-present cigarette that dangled from his lips. His shop was just up the street from a butcher who advertised horse meat for sale; the sign stayed for years, long after they'd stopped selling it.

Until 1970, you had to be older than twenty-one to drink alcohol when the

5 Jak King, *The Drive: A History to 1956* (Vancouver, BC: The Drive Press, 2011), 62.

legal age was dropped to nineteen. Those who were even younger but looked reasonably old enough might drink their first beers down at the American Hotel on Main or in one of the bars in Chinatown that didn't ask for ID—unless it was a Sunday when all the liquor stores and bars were closed, leaving the more adventurous to head to Point Roberts across the border in Washington State.

Keith Singer, who was born in 1951 and raised in East Vancouver where his father was known in the local billiard halls as a pool hustler, recalls that there was a sense of stagnation in East Vancouver that especially affected neighbourhood youth. "There wasn't a lot to do or places to go in this area of town. East Van was a working-class area that had started to run down. There were a lot of older businesses and older homes, but there wasn't a lot to do if you didn't have a job or went to school. [The local secondary schools] Vancouver Technical and Gladstone weren't known as academic schools or strong in athletics [programs]. So a lot of kids had a lot of time on their hands. If you quit school, you had even more time to kill. Put this together with the drug culture that had spread in the area and you have a cultural time bomb."

Rod MacDonald, who grew up south of Clark Park in the 1960s and later worked as a battalion chief with the Vancouver Fire Department, remembers the divide in the city: "The difference between the east side and west side was very noticeable back then. I remember, we went on a visit to a west side school, and everything was nicer, modern, and new there, where our school was really rundown. That sort of thing, that the west side was better off, helped build our dislike [of west siders]. Where we were from, everything was so worse off."

It would be disingenuous to characterize East Van's social problems as approaching anything like the level of urban decay taking place in larger cities at the time, especially in the United States; this was not the South Bronx, after all. There were no depopulated blocks or boarded-up, burnt-out buildings lying in rubble, or drunks passed out or dead on Commercial Drive. But some of the same symptoms of poverty, substance abuse, and absentee parents, combined with North America-wide trends in music, youth counter-culture attitudes, and fashion, contributed to the likelihood of East Vancouver kids joining territorial street gangs as in other cities.

Many East Van youths also shared the experience of having immigrant families. "There was a common denominator in that all our parents were from other ethnicities or countries," remembers Al Walker, who later, as a full-time musician and prominent blues-rock guitarist with his born-and-raised-in-the-East-End roots, played hundreds of gigs in neighbourhood clubs as he came up in the scene. Born in 1956, he grew up in East Vancouver and attended Gladstone secondary school. "There weren't just Italian families, but Scottish, Irish, Portuguese, Eastern European ... My father had come from South Africa. But one thing everybody seemed to have in common were parents who came from somewhere else, where they'd been poor or left for political reasons. Living in this new country, they'd constantly warn us not to get in trouble—so much so, it drove us crazy."

Some parents were overly worried about their kids, but there were others who seemed unable to care for their children at all. These parents, who had lived through the war, were perhaps too preoccupied just trying to put their lives back together to deal with the rest of the world, including their kids. Whether beset with chronic unemployment, poverty, or alcoholism, this story would be repeated time and time again by many East Vancouver families. All too often the boys who lived in such homes learned to shut up before they could talk, and home life seemed constantly filled with tension. Sometimes an absentee mother didn't see her children enough to take care of them; in other cases, it was a nightly guessing game to determine the father's state of drunkenness: would he be tipsy and thus in a good mood, or would the demon drink turn Dad into a minotaur and the home a labyrinth where the boys were chased and beaten, leaving their mothers or sisters lying curled up on the floor? The nightmare of the evening before was never spoken of the next day. "You had hard-working, hard-drinking people," Rod MacDonald recalls. "There was more than one kid out on the street at eleven o'clock at night. If your parents were awake, sometimes you just didn't go home."

Another East Ender, Rod Schnob, recalled his turbulent home life years later in a letter from Matsqui prison where he was serving a life sentence. "The kids on my block jumped me and beat me up pretty good ... I ran home with tears in my eyes and [my father] leaned down and told me that cowards don't live in this house ... [My grandmother] armed me with a stick and a garbage can lid in order to make my presence known to the neighbourhood kids." The only time his father expressed pride in him was when Rod came home wear-

Houses along Heatley Avenue, 1972.
PHOTO: Walter E. Frost, City of Vancouver Archives, CVA 677-947

ing the neighbours' son's blood on his clothes.[6] In such homes, the boys often learned the particular vocabulary of male violence, handed down from father to son. And while once they were too small to defend their mothers or sisters, eventually they became old enough, big enough, and skilled enough to fight back.

Born in Nova Scotia in 1954, Malcolm "Mac" Ryan was another East Vancouver teen with an unstable home life. School life was no less turbulent; disciplined on too many occasions for fighting, vandalism, swearing, and possession of alcohol, he became too much to handle, even for East Van teachers used to dealing with disruptive youth, and he was expelled from the district's schools. "About three or four of us got kicked out of all the East Van schools altogether, so we had to go to Kitsilano Secondary School [on the west side]. What a culture shock!" He laughs when recalling this. "From all the greasers to all the hersheys—that's what we used to call guys from good homes who had better clothes. We had cut-off jackets and tattoos and Dayton boots."

6 Rod Schnob, "Dear Mother, Dear Mother," The Incarcerated InkWell, http://theincarceratedinkwell.ca/

Now in his early sixties, Ryan is a likeable, raffish character with a good sense of humour and a gravelly laugh. He strikes you as the sort of man who worked in the trades for most of his life—but in a trade that may not have always been above-board. He still lives in East Vancouver and is a storehouse of names and stories from decades of living there, periodically interrupted by stays in prison, which began at an early age.

"My stepdad was a real bastard," says Ryan. "He used to beat me and my mother. So eventually, I just ran away from home, and I ended up getting sent to juvie at twelve years old."

Ryan didn't know it, but he was headed to a place that thousands of Vancouver's young offenders would pass through and where many Clark Park gang members would first meet. Vancouver's Juvenile Detention Home was where some of the most unmanageable kids were sent to be disciplined—and for more than just not saying their prayers or combing their hair.

TWO: THE JDH

It's long been a rule of thumb to keep society's troublemakers as far away as possible from its decent citizenry. In Vancouver, as in other cities, most prisons, reform schools, or juvenile detention homes were built at the far reaches of the city limits, then eventually torn down and built even farther away as the city grew. However, in almost all cases, these institutions operated for far longer than they were properly inhabitable or useful.

For several decades, most young women who had run afoul of the law were taken to the Provincial Industrial School for Girls at 868 Cassiar Street. From 1914, when it opened, to 1937, 600 girls aged eight to eighteen from all over BC were incarcerated there for crimes such as incorrigibility, vagrancy, or association with a criminal. A 1954 newspaper report painted a grim picture of the school. The girls were lumped together as inmates, "from the wayward child to the prostitute, drug addict, alcoholic, or mentally ill." In another ward, "sick or homosexual girls are isolated." A group of solitary confinement cells in the basement were noted to be particularly "dungeon-like," with just a mattress and blanket on a damp floor. They were all surely sad places, lacking adequate management, where inmates' problems were ascribed to lack of sufficient discipline or blamed on now-archaic symptoms like "tired blood."[7]

Hospitality wasn't much different in the institutions for Vancouver's young male offenders. From 1910 to 1930, they were sent to places such as the Juvenile Detention Home (JDH), a simple, three-storey building that didn't necessarily evoke a house of correction, located off Pine and West 10th streets, or the Boys Industrial School near 4th and Wallace streets that housed boys ages nine to nineteen.

Problems at the Boys School drew the attention of the press in 1918. *The Daily World* reported on a grand jury investigation that found that the facility was "dirty and unsanitary, cheerless and depressing," and that the children were victims of discipline from one particularly brutal guard who choked and beat them with a stick. It made a strong recommendation to abolish the solitary

7 "BC Delinquent Girls Housed in Damp Cells," *Calgary Herald*, November 11, 1954, 6.

confinement cells "calculated to manufacture criminals or lunatics."[8]

A year later, the building was condemned. But the Point Grey site could not shake the grim ghosts of its past when the building became repurposed as a school for deaf, mute, and blind children called Jericho Hill. As blogger and civic historian Lani Russwurm notes, "Allegations of rampant childhood sexual abuse began surfacing in 1982 at Jericho Hill, and the province shut it down a decade later. After another twelve years of minimizing and downplaying the abuse, the provincial government finally agreed to spend more than $15 million to compensate Jericho Hill school victims in 2004."[9]

While a new boys' reform school had opened in Essondale Hospital (later to become Riverview), and girls were taken to the newer facilities at the Willingdon School for Girls after it opened in 1959, for decades young male offenders were sent to the Juvenile Detention Home off Wall Street in Burrard View Park. Built in 1924 by city architect Arthur Julius Bird, like Jericho Hill, the site had its own ghosts. It was previously the site of the Wall Street Orphanage, which had closed after a 1927 British Columbia child welfare report found that the Vancouver Children's Aid Society was housing children in a building condemned as a fire risk. Foster homes were found for the orphans, the building was demolished, and the Juvenile Detention Hall constructed. By the 1940s, the JDH endured a scandal of its own as a result of overcrowding in its cells.[10]

This reformatory, with its imposing architecture and design that had gone unchanged since the 1930s, would be where a young Mac Ryan, just twelve years old, arrived in 1966. "The first time I got sent in, I was scared shitless. I was really young, and I didn't know anybody," Ryan recalls. JDH inmates were kept in individual cells, woken up early, given strict schedules that involved some schooling, and delegated various chores that kept them busy during the day.

Next to the JDH building that housed the delinquent youth stood a smaller one-storey building that was Vancouver's first family court. The courthouse itself had been constructed on the back of the building that was once the Wall Street Orphanage in Burrard View Park, and is now a hospice centre. The fam-

8 "Grand Jury Finds Conditions in Boys Industrial Home Appalling," *Vancouver Daily World*, December 13, 1918, 1.

9 "Boys Industrial School 1920," http://pasttensevancouver.tumblr.com/

10 Leslie T. Foster and Brian Wharf, eds., *People, Politics, and Child Welfare in British Columbia* (Vancouver, BC: UBC Press, 2007), 13, 16.

ily court was tasked with specifically handling child protection and family maintenance cases, as well as those that fell under the Juvenile Delinquents Act.

The Juvenile Detention home in 1934. The building went unchanged over the years, and as late as the mid-1970s delinquent children were sent there. "Juvie" would be where many future gang members first met.
PHOTO: Stuart Thompson, City of Vancouver Archives, 99-4698

"When I first started to practice law, I spent nearly every day there," says provincial court judge Justice Thomas Gove, who early in his career specialized in the area of family law. Gove recalls that delinquents housed there who faced charges would be escorted by university student-aged guards through a tunnel that connected the cells of the JDH to the courthouse. "They were young, athletic guys, some of them football players—just in jeans and T-shirts. They weren't staff from BC Corrections—they had no uniforms, and nobody had guns or anything like that. They brought the accused kids into the courtroom, usually a few at a time, lining them up on a low bench, like for a basketball team on the sidelines," he says, also noting that none of the youths were ever handcuffed, even though quite a few of them were charged with robberies and violent crimes.

"Occasionally, one of them would try to run away—and when they did, one of the young guards would have to run out of the courtroom to chase after him," Gove says. "One day I was there for a case, and a kid ran, just bolted for the front door, and one of the guards chased and tackled him outside in the parking lot. The kid had got a little bloodied up getting tackled and wanted to go to the hospital, but the guards just dusted him off, told him he was fine, and marched him back into the courthouse. It was always a pretty vivid and interesting scene there."

For those found guilty, the lengths of their sentences were often based on how long before the young offenders became adults. Therefore, it didn't always matter what the crime was; you could potentially be sent away for years. "So if you were caught for shoplifting at age thirteen, you theoretically could remain in custody—unless the staff had determined you had reformed—until you turned an adult, which at that time was considered aged twenty-one. I guess they figured it was good for them to keep them in there for years," Gove says, shaking his head incredulously. "Not many who got sentenced that young had to remain jailed for years, but it could and did happen that delinquents received unnecessarily long sentences."

Furthermore, another section of the Juvenile Delinquents Act allowed parents to go to the court and claim that their child was beyond their control. If the court agreed, the child could be arrested, brought to court, and sent off to juvenile detention, never having actually been arrested for a specific crime. Gove recalls that these cases were much less common, and when they did fall on the juvenile court dockets, they most often involved delinquent girls. "Their parents usually complained that they were hanging out with an older boy who was no good for them, and their daughter would no longer listen to them," he says.

As for the young males in juvenile detention, "A lot of them were in for burglaries, fighting, or stealing cars," Gove says, "but these weren't kids chopping up the cars for parts to resell, or sending them on freighters overseas for profit. They were stealing cars to commit a robbery with them, or just going for joyrides. I remember one kid was in there on and off quite a bit for stealing cars and then driving or pushing them off a hill or a ravine, just to see the cars crash at the bottom. So this wasn't organized crime—it was just crime or violence for the sake of doing it."

Gove admits that by the early 1970s it was quite commonly accepted among those who worked around the courts that the JDH was an archaic institution; it began to be viewed as an unacceptable place to house delinquents. But for

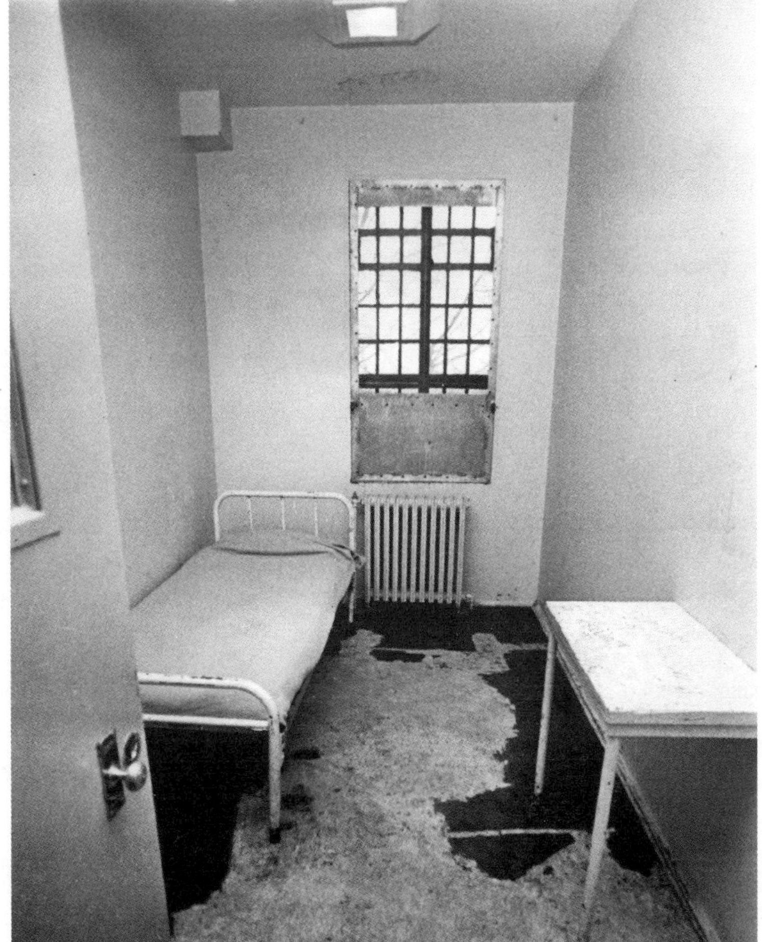

A cell inside the JDH.
PHOTO: Gordon Croucher, *The Province*, 1972

those who experienced a disruptive life at home, the JDH would often be perceived as a welcome respite.

"I can still remember my first morning there," recalls Mac Ryan. "After they got us up, I went down to the cafeteria for breakfast. At home, all I had was shitty powdered milk and lousy food. But there on each table they had big pitchers of milk—real homogenized milk!" he laughs. "There were four different types of cereal, toast and jam, apples and oranges. I couldn't believe it! I ate a bowl of cereal and pushed my bowl away figuring that was all we were allowed to have, and a kid next to me says, 'Have some more.' I said, 'Holy shit, you're allowed to have more?' Lunch was good, too. Dinner was beautiful."

But when he was released, life at home had not improved, and Ryan repeatedly found himself being sent back to juvenile detention. "Maybe because the food was good, I kept subconsciously going back," Ryan jokes. For years he would repeat a pattern of avoiding home, crashing with friends, and after getting arrested for a new string of burglaries and offences, being sent back to the JDH. "I practically grew up there—it was like my second home. I stopped counting after twenty times. Between the ages of twelve and seventeen, I must have been sentenced there twenty-five times."

There were so many East Vancouver youths in Juvenile Detention that the guards had to split them into two shifts during recreation or sports hours (murder ball was a favourite game), as the East Vancouver boys were deemed too problematic to be let out of their cells all at once. Even then, altercations were not uncommon. In 1968, when Ryan was fourteen, he got into a fight started by another boy in the JDH. While defending himself, he broke the boy's nose and was put in solitary confinement—a narrow cell with a steel-plate door.

A typical stint in solitary lasted a few days to a week and was usually doled out only to the more mature boys in detention. But Ryan was kept in solitary for six weeks. "I went fucking nuts in there. When the head of the JDH found out from the bulls [JDH guards] that I'd been in there that long, I heard him screaming in his office at them, 'You can't keep somebody in there that long, especially a young kid like that!'" No one at the JDH was reprimanded for Ryan's unreasonably long seclusion in solitary.

Boys who were too problematic or repeat offenders, like Ryan, were eventually sent right out of the city. "In 1970, I got sent to the Brannen Lake jail outside of Nanaimo on Vancouver Island," Ryan recalls. "They walked me right out of the JDH with an escort guard and down across the street to Burrard Inlet where the float planes were that took you over there." When they got in the plane, the guard handcuffed Ryan to the seat. "I said, 'What if this thing goes down? What am I supposed to do, for chrissake?' And he says to me, 'If this thing goes down, you're finished anyway.'"

Ryan spent three months at Brannen Lake, a large institution run by the province that at its height housed about 200 boys. But his stay there did little for him except introduce him to older and/or more serious offenders who had come from all over BC with lawbreaking skills that they were more than happy to pass along to their young pupils. Ryan would graduate, so to speak, when he left with a BISCO cross tattoo. "BISCO stood for Boys Industrial School for Criminal Offenders, which is [what we] called the place." He still has the tattoo on his hand, to symbolize the time he did in the jail.

After numerous stays in detention, Ryan began to recognize a number of familiar faces of those who, like himself, had been in and out of reformatories over the years. There was, in fact, seemingly little reforming going on in such places. In juvenile detention halls, younger offenders were more apt to learn new criminal skills and make new connections, including Ryan, who made friends on the inside with a number of juvenile offenders from East Vancouver.

"One day, this kid I'd seen around in the JDH was in the cell next to me and said, 'Ryan, where do you hang out?' I told him I was mostly in South Vancouver with some guys I knew down there, and he said, 'Do yourself a favour, and when you get out of here come to 14th and Commercial. That's where the Clark Park gang is. If you've got the jam, that is.' I had heard of them, heard about their tough reputation. I told him 'I don't know if I want to go up there.' He just laughed and said, 'Just tell him Gavin sent you. Gerry Gavin. I'll probably be there.'"

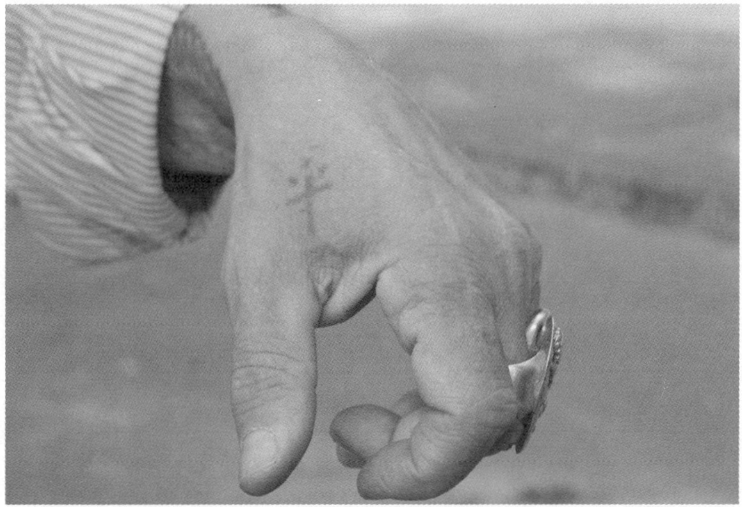

The BISCO Cross tattoo on the hand of Mac Ryan. The tattoo was earned because he'd done time at the Boys Industrial School for Criminal Offenders, where typically only the most incorrigible and unmanageable young men were sent.
PHOTO: Erik Iversen, 2016

THREE: RUMBLE

The word "gang" has been so widely and sensationally used by police, media, and popular culture over the years to define such a broad range of criminals that everything from a loose affiliation of street urchins dabbling in mischief and pickpocketing to organized criminal operations with international connections involved in drug trafficking and murder are given the "gang" label. The first time the word was used in print in Vancouver is over 100 years ago, when it appeared in the November 23, 1909, edition of *The Province*. The article noted that police identified and apprehended a "gang" following a series of house burglaries and reported that the home of Mrs. Keddy at 699 Cambie Street "was robbed of furs, silverware and $20 in cash."

But specifically, youth-gang activities in the city appear to increase in the 1920s. Vancouver's first recognized gangs were largely made up of orphaned street kids and dropouts who travelled in packs. Little is known about these gangs aside from what was reported in the newspapers of the period. With names like the Collingwood Street gang or the Homer Street gang, they were comprised of boys aged eleven to twenty who, given to loitering on street corners, harassed passersby and engaged in automobile theft, arson, vandalism, and often violent robberies of local businesses. Their activities left a disgusted public—especially senior members of the community, who were often repeat victims—calling for increases in criminal prosecutions.

The gangs were, at the very least, a nuisance to police and the court system. But if caught by police, these young offenders were often turned back over to the discipline of their parents, if the parents could be found at all. Juvenile detention facilities of the time were typically overburdened and reserved for the worst of the bad apples. In some cases, the parents of the young gang members may have even been harsher or more vicious in their punishments than the court sentences and reformatory schools might offer.

In comparison with much of the youth violence we hear about today, it's easy to dismiss the gangs of the past as no more than rowdy, misguided, boys-will-be-boys street hoodlums whose activities were more like hijinks that got out of hand than that of violent marauders with a malevolent agenda. But while the street gangs of the past were poorly organized, and there are no records showing that they committed any murders, it's worth noting that they were often armed, and the potential for violence was always high. For example, in 1935, the Silk Stocking gang was involved in a store robbery where the proprietor was shot and wounded. Elmer Almquist, gang member responsible for the shooting, was an adult, and sentenced to seven years in prison.[11]

By the war-torn 1940s, while Vancouver had grown considerably, the ranks of the Vancouver police had been depleted of young constables with so many men going overseas. Most of the officers were World War I veterans or men now too old to serve in combat. The war years helped to create the next distinct era of Vancouver gangs, one with the soundtrack of a big-band playing bebop.

The Vancouver Zoot Suit Riot during the summer heat wave of 1944 might be the most fabled, when mobs of civilians and members of the Zoot Suit gang fought against visiting merchant marine sailors on city streets over the course of three nights. One skirmish that took place near Granville and Smithe streets involved hundreds of people; it had to be broken up by military police.

Unlike the gangs that had preceded them which had no distinctive uniforms, "Zooters" had "their own specialized vocabulary, they wore large waist-length, square shouldered jackets, [and] baggy trousers called 'strides' that were tight at the ankle."[12]

Newspapers of the time loved to repeat the sensational highlights of the riot. But the term "Zoot Suiter" may not have even accurately applied to Vancouver's gang. The news of their presence in Vancouver followed the much publicized Zoot Suit Riots in Los Angeles in 1943, and the press in Vancouver may have jumped on the term to describe the local hoodlums who frequented and caused trouble at dance halls, cafés, and certain nightspots at closing time. To some, like Alan Morley writing in the *News-Herald*, their name didn't matter; the "Zoot Suiters" were no different from "the perennial succession of East End gangs that ... Vancouver's slums have always bred."[13]

By 1950, Vancouver Police had identified twenty-seven gang meeting places or

11"Long Terms Imposed on Holdup Men," *The Province*, October 21, 1935, 1.

12 Michael G. Young, "History of Vancouver Youth Gangs" (master's thesis, Simon Fraser University, 1993), 42.

13 Lani Russwurm, "Street Fighting Man." Past Tense Vancouver Histories, November 12, 2009. https://pasttensevancouver.wordpress.com/tag/clark-park-gang/

hangouts that ranged from pool halls to coffee bars and street corners, and an investigation revealed that one unidentified gang was making its own crude weapons, including "a gas pipe blackjack, wooden clubs, and chains."[14] The '50s opened the switchblade and greaser decade of Vancouver youth gangs. Automobiles gave them wider access to the city, and inter-gang rumbles and street racing were coined "Friday Night Madness," which was viewed with the same trepidation, and accompanied by a similar increase in police presence, that "Welfare Wednesday" has in recent years.

North Vancouver, 1958.
PHOTO: Fred Herzog

The post-war era seemed to give rise to a new fear of street gangs. The very mention of the word "gang" captured newspaper headlines in Vancouver and abroad, ready to scare suburbia with a nightmare vision that lawless youth at any time were waiting to roar up your driveway in a hot rod, smash in the front door, and rape your family. Gangs became scapegoats for unidentified or unsolved crimes even when there was no evidence to indicate gang involvement. BC senator Tom Reid saw the Red Menace of Communism lurking behind the perceived new wave of youth gang violence, and told press that "gang members were the most susceptible to Communist doctrine and thus easy prey for recruitment drives."[15]

14 Young, 55.
15 "Vicious Hoodlums Rob, Wreck House," *The Province*, February 2, 1952, 2.

This period in Vancouver was not without gang-related criminal incidents, particularly when it came to the animosity between east and west side rivals. A gang called the Alma Dukes, which was based on the west side around Broadway and Alma streets and boasted a membership of 400, had been named by Vancouver police in an extensively reported rumble with an east side rival named the Victoria Road gang, which had 150 male and some female members of their own.

By 1952, Vancouver police chief Walter Mulligan declared that the Alma Dukes and other gangs had been eradicated thanks to a "Youth Guidance Detail."[16] But Mulligan's boast that he'd wiped out local street gangs was as short-lived as his own career; he famously fell from grace three years later in the wake of a sensational bribery and corruption scandal that forced his resignation.

The 1960s and '70s would bring on a new era of gang trouble. Some of the gangs in Vancouver were not territorial street thugs; their activities more closely resembled the workings of organized crime. Rumours swirled in those years about an Italian mafia presence in Vancouver. Names frequently bantered around included Joe Gentile, a local mob connection who ran his operation exceedingly quietly, and members of the Filippone family of Penthouse Nightclub fame who many simply assumed to be connected to the underworld because they were Italians who had publicly skirted liquor and prostitution laws for decades. It was known, however, that the Palmer brothers and William "Fats" Robertson were involved in Vancouver's organized crime scenes.

The Palmers were blue-collar heroin dealers with connections to the Montreal mafia.[17] They drank at the Waldorf Hotel bar on East Hastings Street but distanced themselves from the possibility of arrest by avoiding handling drug transactions directly. Instead, they sold small maps to where "nickel" and "dime" bags (five and ten dollars' worth) of drugs were stashed in the alleyways of East Vancouver.

Fats Robertson had been involved in Vancouver's criminal history since the 1940s, and had been linked to everything from trafficking and robbery to murder. His criminal career in the murky depths of the Lower Mainland's underworld eventually included dirty trading in the stock market.

Concern over gang violence involving young offenders in the city rose in July of

16 Robert Hertzler, "Vancouver's Juvenile Gangs 'Wiped Out' in Two Years," *Spokane Daily Chronicle*, March 17, 1952, 12.
17 "7 On Drug Conspiracy Charges," *The Province*, June 24, 1972, 2.

1962 when two female Vancouver police constables, responding to a report of a gang fight outside the Danceland Ballroom at Hornby and Robson streets, were forced to seek the safety of their police cruiser after gang members threatened them. While a crowd of about 300 gathered to watch, ten gang members took hold of the car's rear bumper and tried to tip it over until the backup officers finally arrived to break up the scene and make arrests.[18] The following year, constables Ted Urchenko and R.L. Kirkland were arresting a drunken youth gang member on West Broadway when they were attacked by ten other members of the gang while trying to place him in their patrol vehicle. Urchenko was knocked unconscious. While Kirkland radioed for reinforcements and an ambulance, the youth fled to nearby cars and escaped.[19]

These incidents hit the front pages of the local newspapers, increasing concern over youth gangs to new heights. And while it's difficult to trace an exact moment when the "park gang" era began, many gangs were already being identified according to their community of origin or territory, which often centred around community parks. By 1963, *The Province* reported on a skirmish at Grandview Park where more than eighty juveniles had rallied to engage in a rumble by the time police had arrived to disperse the crowd.[20] Clark Park was one of several city parks that police had regularly named in the newspapers that year as a street gang hangout.

For many years, Vancouver residents slept easily, knowing that the greaser gangs, as well as those in organized crime, were usually too busy warring amongst themselves to pose much of a threat to the general public. But the street gangs—influenced by changing attitudes of youth and counterculture, revolt against the establishment, a lack of respect for law enforcement, and a dismissal of what had previously been considered societal standards—would clash directly with the police in full view of the public in Vancouver in a way that had never been seen before.

Ross Park in South Vancouver covers about 1.5 hectares (almost four acres), and in the late 1960s and early 1970s was part of a low-to-middle-class neighbourhood. The park was surrounded by one- or two-storey rancher homes built

18 "Policewomen Saved from Teen-Age Mob," *The Province*, July 9, 1962, 1.
19 "4 Policemen Hurt in Gang Attacks by Young Hoodlums," *Vancouver Sun*, February 25, 1963, 3.
20 "Hoodlums Beat, Kick Two Men," *The Province*, July 30, 1963, 27; "Gangs Attack Three in the City," *The Province*, December 15, 1963, 15.

in the 1940s and '50s, as well as the new, box-like stucco "Vancouver Specials" that were beginning to be built and would become a staple of East and South Vancouver neighbourhoods.

Brothers Destry and Louis Galgoczy grew up in the area in the 1960s and were no different than many of the local youth hanging around Ross Park at the time, often well after the sun had gone down. "We had hung out at Ross Park since we were kids," Destry explains. "We were around twelve years old, but there was also

Members of the Riley Park gang.
PHOTO: Dan Scott, *Vancouver Sun*, 1974

a crowd of older teenagers ... who hung out there too, sort of showing us the ropes." He and his friends would try to bum liquor or cigarettes off the older kids, or simply follow their lead.

Perhaps too young to be considered full-fledged Ross Park gang members themselves, they nonetheless socialized as young hangers-on with the older youths there. "A lot of the older kids were in gangs," he says. "The Riley Park gang, Sunset Park gang, and Ross Park gang all sort of had allegiances to one another because we were all in South Van, so the territory from 33rd to Victoria Drive and over to Main Street was all considered part of 'our territory.'"

One early fall evening in 1971, Destry and his brother arrived as usual at Ross Park to find an altogether different mood. "When we got there, we knew something was up. The older guys had all shown up on their motorcycles or in cars if they had them. An older guy, Don Garrett, came up to us and told us we had to get out of there right now, that there was going to be a rumble."

Just then, swearing and shouting could be heard in the distance as another couple dozen older teenagers marched into the park from the east. They were long-haired and wore red mackinaw jackets (macks), some with the sleeves cut off, and a jean jacket over top, with jeans and Dayton boots. It was too late for the Galgoczy brothers to run off, so Garrett pushed the two boys on top of the roof of the field house and told them to wait there and stay quiet. "We just sat up there and hid," remembers Louis. "Then these guys started squaring off. I didn't see any knives, but people were hitting each other with bats and chains, right in the corner of Ross Park. All hell broke loose. It's amazing how violent people were back then."

Neighbours in the homes that surrounded Ross Park might have sat in their darkened living rooms that night, bathed in the reflected glow of their Zenith Electrohome TVs, perhaps mistaking the yells from outside as noisy kids playing in the park. Maybe they only grimaced and turned up the volume. Others who got up to peer through their blinds perhaps did nothing further. Even the driver of a passing car glimpsing such a fight might be too intimidated to stop and break up something like this on his own. Many who lived around city parks, especially older residents, chose to avoid any confrontations with local youths, and told their own children to stay out of the parks after dark.

Some braver residents, however, would telephone police to report fighting in the park. But unless officers were already in the area, they would rarely arrive upon a fight still in progress, as the warning sounds of a police siren would cause the gang members to flee down nearby alleys and pathways.

That night in Ross Park, however, hiding on the rooftop of the clubhouse, the Galgoczy brothers kept their heads down low as they witnessed the fight, hearing the swearing and beating as the brutal rumble unfolded.

"We knew who it was. We'd heard about them," Destry says. "We knew they were from a tough park. It was the guys from the east end. The Clark Parkers."

FOUR: THE GOOD OLD BAD OLD DAYS

You could say that there was always something crooked about Clark Park—and not just the downhill slope of the park ground itself. Vancouverites had been wary of Clark Park from its beginnings.

The park sits at what was once the end of Park Drive, a road carved out of the forests as a logging trail that ran north to the Burrard Inlet near the original site of Hastings Mill where the city of Vancouver itself began. It is the second oldest park in Vancouver after the larger and internationally known Stanley Park. Park Drive cut through an area that eventually would be known as Grandview—one of the city's oldest neighbourhoods. Before European settlers arrived, and long before it was logged in the 1890s, Squamish First Nations communities lived in the area for many hundreds of years, referring to the region as Khupkhahpay'ay (meaning "cedar tree"). The area maintains a strong First Nations presence to this day, with one in ten residents identifying as Aboriginal.[21]

The city's most plainly told and superficial history would simply state that the Park came into being when, in 1889, Mr. E.J. Clark—a dry goods baron who had turned his profits toward real estate acquisition—graciously donated the land he'd purchased just a few years earlier to the city's newly created Park Commission. For reasons that no one seems to recall, it was first known as Buffalo Park or South Park; senior Vancouverites who had grown up and lived in the area well into the 1960s continued to call it by either name.

But the whole story of the land grant can't be explained as solely emanating from the warm-hearted generosity of a local citizen who, once he'd done well, desired to give back to his burgeoning coastal town. Clark was also a shrewd businessman who felt there was more profit to be gained from giving the land away. Clark had donated it to the city with conditions attached: it

21 Stevie Wilson, "You Should Know: The History of the City's Grandview-Woodland Neighbourhood." Scout Magazine, May 23, 2013. http://scoutmagazine.ca/2013/05/23/you-should-know-the-history-of-the-citys-grandview-woodland-neighbourhood/

should be cleared of stumps and roots, and the ground be ploughed and levelled. He hoped that the attractions of Buffalo Park would become a feature of the area and would benefit his other property taking up some twenty-five hectares (sixty acres) that he continued to own and intended to sell for home development.[22]

By 1904, despite its official designation as a city park, it was not much in demand for recreational or athletic activities. Park Drive was a well-used road and even had a terminus stop for the streetcar line that ran hourly. And the local population did not significantly increase: too much of the city was still focused downtown and near Burrard Inlet.

While a small portion of the park was left as a virgin forest, much of it had become covered with weeds and bracken. At one time, city engineers had to remind the park board that it was still in their possession.[23] Dissatisfied with the way the park had yet to help develop any real estate interests, E.J. Clark's nephew William Clark insisted that the city had breached its conditions and reneged on its responsibility. He demanded that the park be given back to the family. He sued the city and fought the case all the way to the Supreme Court of Canada, but ultimately lost the trial.[24]

Yet E.J. Clark perhaps had the last laugh. When he originally donated the land, he also had the surrounding area surveyed into lots, accounting for streets and lanes, which he sold. The lots eventually changed hands many times, but there was little development. By 1907, when the construction of homes began to take off, builders who applied to the city for a water connection were notified by Clark that they were trespassing on his property. Either by accident or design, one foot (30.5 cm) of each street end and lane was still the registered property of Clark himself, who stated that he did not intend to relinquish his claim on the one-foot strips without adequate recompense. He even asked for fifteen dollars per lot before he would allow the streets and lanes to be opened to the city.[25]

The story hit the local newspapers and even as far east as Quebec, as readers of the *Montreal Gazette* were amused to read of Vancouver's real estate fiascos.

22 "A Real Estate Dodge," *Montreal Gazette*, June 27, 1907, 9.
23 Richard (Mike) Steele, *The First 100 Years: An Illustrated Celebration* (Vancouver, BC: Vancouver Board of Parks and Recreation, 1988), 41.
24 *Clark v. City of Vancouver*, [1904] 35 S.C.R. 121.
25 "A Real Estate Dodge," *Montreal Gazette*, June 27, 1907, 9.

It forced a city council hearing after which the various home owners and Clark were all eventually placated with a negotiated settlement. The home owners got their water tie-ins, and despite the bad blood between the Clarks and the city, Vancouver would officially rename the greenspace Clark Park in 1911. That same year, an effort begun by area merchants in the hopes of attracting businesses to Park Drive would succeed in having it renamed to what it is today: Commercial Drive. (The Clark Park gang might thank the Vancouver Park Board for this: The Buffalo Park Gang or South Park Gang doesn't have the same ring!)

In 1923, the Chambers family of East Vancouver gathered on the slope of Clark Park to take a photograph.
PHOTO: Stuart Thompson, City of Vancouver Archives, CVA 99-3460

By 1912, Grandview had begun to grow as a distinct village east of downtown, and the area within walking distance of Commercial Drive became filled with new homes. As the neighbourhood grew, Clark Park finally became more of a feature in the larger area and recognized as a recreational spot for East Vancouver families to enjoy on a pleasant day at an outdoor music concert or to take a family photo. The Chambers family was not unlike most of their neighbours; a broader wave of multicultural immigration was yet to show itself in the neighbourhood. Residents then were predominantly of British ancestry, as indicated by such local names as Britannia Secondary School, Queen Victoria Elementary, and Victoria Drive.

But after more than four decades had passed since George Chambers had his family photo taken in Clark Park, an altogether different group of people started gathering there.

Not long after he left juvenile detention again, waving to the guards on his way out the door and promising that, this time, he'd be a model citizen, Mac Ryan took Gerry Gavin up on his invitation—albeit with some trepidation—to go to Clark Park.

Entering off the Commercial Drive entrance and walking up the crest of the hill, Ryan could hear the noise before he saw what was going on—the sounds of voices as if a party were underway. "I came up the hill, and I couldn't believe it. I saw about twenty, maybe twenty-five guys there," he says. "I was a bit scared shitless. I stopped for a second and thought maybe I should turn around and get out of there. But Gavin was there along with other guys like Paul Melo and Chief, whom I'd known in Juvie too, and they called me over. They introduced me around to everybody. And that was it."

Clark Park itself, as remembered by neighbours and reports of the time, was less hospitable than it is today; it was more rundown, with more litter, broken glass, and bottle caps along its paths. E.J. Clark would likely have spun in his grave if he could see what his imagined verdant, pleasant city park had become by 1970.

To any passersby who might have walked through the park that day, the group that Mac Ryan met might have appeared as a bunch of scruffy older teenagers—smoking, drinking, and loitering in the park—not much more than a neighbourhood nuisance. But this collection of East Vancouver boys would not only go on to run amok like no youth gang in the city before them, but as they matured and graduated to more serious crimes, both individually and as a group, they created a wave throughout the British Columbia judicial and correctional system for years to come.

Gary Blackburn had been a regular at Clark Park long before Mac Ryan arrived. "There was an older group of Clark Parkers there before us," he recalled. "Guys like Larry Jang who lived near the park. They were an earlier generation who'd hung out [there] since the early 1960s. But they kept to themselves because most of them just lived in that immediate neighbourhood and didn't venture out. They told us stories of the hell-raising they did, and sometimes we'd even get into some fights with them. I myself had a very bad temper back then," Blackburn admits.

Born in 1955, today Blackburn is a soft-spoken, lean figure with an air of cautiousness, perhaps a result of that bad temper which not only got him out of some tight spots, but put him in just as many. As a teenager, he too had found himself in the JDH after being caught for stealing cars and breaking and entering. "That's how we made our money," he says matter-of-factly. "When you got caught and ended up in juvenile detention or at Brannen Lake [jail]—those places amalgamated everybody. If you didn't know them already from around East Vancouver, you sure got to meet them there."

Gary Blackburn (left) and Bradley Bennett, early 1970s.
PHOTO: Courtesy of Bradley Bennett

Blackburn recalls how the ranks of the park gangs were filled by those he'd met in juvenile detention. "Back then all these different regions of town had their own gangs, and a lot of them were our enemies," he says. "Riley Park gang, Bobolink Park gang, even the Dunbar Park gang out on the west side. But with Clark Park there were people from all over town who made up our thing. We tended to amalgamate the best and the toughest people from other gangs into Clark Park. And after a while, everybody wanted to be a Clark Parker."

Danny "Mouse" Williamson, born in 1953, was one who made the cut. He arrived at Clark Park having been toughened at an early age. He was one-quarter Métis on his mother's side, and largely had a good relationship with her. He was not as lucky with his father. "My dad was an alcoholic and was always telling me not to take shit from anybody," he says. Along with that admonition, Williamson's father gave him his nickname; as a young child, Danny often wore a Mickey Mouse shirt. One day, Williamson invited his Clark Park friends over to his house, and they heard his father call him "Mouse"—and the name stuck. "There are people I've known in East Van for over forty years, and they still call me 'Mouse.' I don't think they even know my real name." But the nickname belied his nature; Williamson was always ready for a fight.

Danny "Mouse" Williamson, who joined the Clark Park gang via the Renfrew Huns. PHOTO: Courtesy of Lana Williamson

Williamson and his family lived in a number of places around the Trout Lake area in East Vancouver. As a teenager he started to hang out with a gang called the Renfrew Park Huns who gained a reputation for wearing Maltese crosses and swastikas that they also sprayed as graffiti on neighbourhood walls. Despite adopting the controversial symbols, this was done for shock value and to upset older people, rather than due to any fascist agenda.

"One day in 1968, the Huns had a rumble with the Clark Park gang, and one of the Clark Parkers whipped one of our guys with a chain," Williamson says. "We broke it up, but in the fight I looked around and realized that I knew all these Clark Parkers from school and the neighbourhood when I was a little kid. So we actually started to hang out a bit, and I came over from the Renfrew Huns to join. I tell you, soon guys came over from Riley Park,

A member of the Catwalkers, a motorcycle gang from the 1950s, is ticketed on Georgia Street for not wearing a helmet. Some of the early biker gangs in Greater Vancouver included the Hades Horsemen, the North Van Rogues, and the Misfits, who all fought with the Clark Park gang. PHOTO: Ross Kenward, *The Province*, 1968

Renfrew Park—a bunch of those guys became Hells Angels years later. It escalated quickly from there. There were gangs before, but not ever like this."

Forty years later, Williamson still maintains a streetwise nature. Looking a bit like an older Matt Dillon, he speaks with a dusky, resonant voice and comes across as a good judge of character, even if he's made a few mistakes over the years. He retains a good memory for the old days, and like many of the other original Clark Park gang, a sense of humour. Now in his early sixties, he's mellowed since his wild younger days, but you get the feeling that he could still easily deal with a dangerous situation.

"Fighting wasn't the only reason behind Clark Park, but we had a lot of tough guys," Williamson says. "We beat up a lot of other gangs in town—even motorcycle gangs like the Hades Horsemen, the Misfits from New Westminster, and the North Van Rogues. Everybody wanted to scrap with us, and we beat them. The only ones we didn't get into fights with were the Satan's Angels because we were friends, and they were like older brothers to us." (The Satan's Angels would later be absorbed into the Hells Angels when they officially arrived in town in the early 1980s.)[26]

By the late 1960s, the Clark Parkers were gaining status. "Anybody that was anybody who wanted to be in a gang gravitated to us," Williamson says. "And it really grew. While there was probably a hard-core group of about fifty or sixty of us, we could get two, three hundred guys together in an hour if we had to. Most of us never had cars, so we'd be left to march through the streets with baseball bats and pieces of picket fences at night, headed somewhere." Gary Blackburn agrees. "There was a lot of fighting back then. Most of the time it was because somebody was trying to bully us or wanted to start something. But we stuck together. Pretty soon it got to be known: if you fuck with one of us, you'd have to fuck with us all."

"In the hierarchy of the parks back then, Clark Park was the pinnacle," says Bradley Bennett, who was born in 1954. Bennett's parents had been divorced for as long as he could remember. As a young adolescent, his mother left him in the care of his grandmother. "The 1960s was happening, fashion was changing. If you wanted to wear different clothes, have longer hair, or do different things, strict English nannies like my old British grandmother just weren't the type to go along with that. And I just wasn't into [obeying her]," Bennett says.

As a teenager, he attended John Oliver Secondary School in East Vancouver where he grew a rebellious streak the length of Commercial Drive. In the 1960s, the punishment for teenage rebellion meant more than losing video game or cell phone privileges for a few days. "Discipline was completely different back then," Bennett says. "I knew some kids my age whose dads had horse whips they'd use on them. Even at school, they'd belt you on your hands or your ass if you got into trouble. I remember kids used to make paddles for the teachers in woodworking class, cutting holes in them for less wind resistance."

Out of school, Bennett spent his days wandering the city and embarking on all manner of enterprises to make a little pocket money. "We used to walk underneath the Granville Street Bridge, steal baby pigeons out of their nests there, and bring them down to Chinatown to sell to the Chinese guys that ran the Green Door restaurant," says Bennett. "He'd give us twenty-five cents apiece, and then the bastard would let us go to the gambling den he ran upstairs and sell us a deck of cards for fifty-two dollars to play solitaire. The

26 Rick Ouston, "It's a 'Frightening Name' but Police Can Cite No Links," *Vancouver Sun*, October 29, 1983.

Bradley Bennett, 1970s.
PHOTO: Courtesy of Bradley Bennett

object of the game was to get all four aces up and then as you went through the deck you tried to get each suit up in numerical order. Every card you got back up on the ace, you won back five bucks. There would be six or seven of us, and with all our pigeon money we'd go in on a deck of cards together, and that motherfucker would win it all back from us." Bennett usually declined to eat at the restaurant. "It wasn't so much the pigeons. There were never any stray animals within a three or four block radius of the Green Door."

In his early Clark Park days, as seen in photographs of the time, Bennett is lanky with red hair and an easy, handsome, roguish grin. While he might have been a menace to society in his younger days, Bennett now seems affable, intelligent, and gregarious, an old-fashioned strong and silent type. He conveys a certain coolness under fire—he has seen much of life—but Bennett also displays a wry sense of humour.

In his young teens, he ran with the Grays Park gang at 33rd and Windsor, but after he quit school and ran away from home, Bennett began to steal cars and break into houses. He landed in juvenile detention where he met Clark Parkers such as Gary Blackburn and Norman Halliban, who later invited him up to Clark Park as Gerry Gavin had with Mac Ryan.

"I was more into disturbing the peace than breaking into houses," Ryan says. "But there was a lot of fighting with other gangs back then. We didn't always get out unscathed. It seemed like I had a black eye myself every month. I remember somebody asking me, 'Hey, who gave you that black eye?', and I told them, 'Nobody gave it to me—I earned it.'" And if the fights and rumbles were

Rick Stuart, 1970s.
PHOTO: Courtesy of Rick Stuart

earning the Clark Parkers a reputation in East Vancouver, it was the robberies and B and Es that were quickly bringing them to the attention of the Vancouver Police Department. "We must have cleaned out East Vancouver," former Clark Parker Rick Stuart says with a guilty laugh. At times, the robberies were concentrated on local businesses. A pizza restaurant at 12th and Renfrew was a favourite target; the gang broke into the shop after hours and took money, cigarettes, or beer that the employees kept there until, after multiple break-ins, the restaurant finally installed an alarm.

The burglaries of residential homes were riskier, and took on a more reckless nature. "I remember we broke into a couple of houses where people weren't home, and we sat down and watched TV, made something to eat, and acted like we lived there," says Mouse Williamson, recalling the darkly comic nature of the scene. On one occasion, Williamson and five other Clark Parkers broke into a home near 29th and Renfrew streets and stole a coin collection with paperwork that put its value at $62,000. Without the connections of professional thieves to fence the coins for their estimated value, the kids "just split it six ways and spent it all at face value," he says. Cash was always the easiest to steal and to get rid of. "The houses with Chinese families were the best," Bennett says. "For some reason, they always kept a lot of cash in the house." The thieves spent their hauls on alcohol, cigarettes, and food.

Alternatively, if they were light on cash, they would "pump gas"—a term for robbing local gas stations that were easy targets, especially in the days before security video cameras were commonplace. One easy score was from a friendly kid who worked as an attendant at the Esso Gas station that once stood at Main Street and Terminal Avenue. "When the police came and asked for a description of who did it, he would just say it was someone that didn't look like us at all," Williamson recalls. "One time when we were robbing [the gas station], the cops came busting through the door, and the kid told the police we were just trying to help him. Talk about a close call."

Inevitably each of the Clark Parkers would be caught for one offence or another, and once again be sent back through the revolving doors of juvenile detention. Some avoided being caught more than others.

Born in 1953, Rick Stuart had attended Gladstone High School and started to hang around Clark Park in 1967. But although he joined the others in various burglaries, he somehow managed to avoid incarceration in juvenile detention or a stay in jail. "The park looks a little different than it did back then," he says. "There were a few more bushes and places to hide. Maybe I just bobbed and weaved better than the others."

Both his father and grandfather were tugboat skippers, and Stuart wanted to join the other men in his family who worked on the water. Finishing his high school education—a requirement for employment on the boats—kept him working and busy, largely avoiding more serious trouble. "I knew some of the other guys from the park like Coke Singh and 'Greasy' Keith Holley, but Mouse and I grew up just a few houses apart," Stuart recalls. "We didn't have a lot of money; our parents used to give us peanut butter and sugar sandwiches back then. My old man was a drunk and enjoyed using the belt for discipline, so some nights I avoided home as much as possible. The one thing we had in common was that none of our families were well off."

With a shaved head, beard, sharp blue eyes, and heavily tattooed arms and back, Rick Stuart might appear intimidating if you met him on the street. But in conversation he reveals himself to be an easy-going character with a ready grin. His time with the Clark Park gang left him with a distaste for the police, but the poverty of East Vancouver in those years is most distinct in his memory. "I remember a crazy guy who was around the park then. His family lived above Ernie's Grocery at Commercial and Salsbury in a two-bedroom suite. There was a bunch of them in there. Their father was a simple sort of guy who hoarded stuff in their home. The bathtub was full of old engine parts. I don't know if they ever showered or cleaned. There were grimy pots on the stove, and there wasn't a clean cup in the house. I don't think some of the kids went to school."

Bradley Bennett recalls the family, too. "The two brothers used to argue and get into fights all the time. One day, they came home from school and the parents had moved away—just packed up and taken everything with them and just left their kids behind. Social services had to come in and take care of them."

For many, the park had simply become an easier and more relaxed place to hang out than their own homes, and many boys found more acceptance from friends than their own kin. Girls who hung out with or dated members of the gang came and went, unless they were sisters of gang members. While there were always female friends and hangers-on, the gang certainly remained a boys' club. "We were all guys born in the 1950s and grew up in those times," Rick Stuart says. "And with our own parents, sometimes the dads came and went. Nobody had very modern views on women. Everybody had to grow up and learn that a lot later."

The makeup of the gang was always changing. "People drifted in and out [of the gang]," Stuart continues. "There wasn't a continuum of the same guys all the time. But one thing that never changed was that there was zero prejudice against anybody. You were who you were, and nobody was better than anybody else." The negligible racism among Clark Parkers could be attributed to the lower-class upbringing that everyone shared; there were members who came from First Nations, Indo-Canadian, and African-Canadian backgrounds.

By the end of the 1960s, "outsiders were starting to say that Clark Park was an evil scary place, and maybe there was some truth to it," Stuart says. "There used to be a field house there next to the wading pool—it's gone now—but they had boxing gloves there we could use. No wonder we got so tough; we were beating the hell out of each other all the time as kids. After a while, nobody could put the fear of God into us. We had done that to each other already."

While many of the Clark Parkers were large for their age or could punch above their weight, Roger Daggitt "was a one-man wrecking crew," says Bradley Bennett. Bennett first met Daggitt and Gary Blackburn in juvenile detention, when Bennett was thirteen. "I don't remember when he was ever small. Even when we were kids, he was always big. At Juvie, he ripped this big metal door in solitary confinement right off its fucking hinges. Just smashed it right off. They had to call the police, who handcuffed him and took him downtown to jail—he was still a juvenile, but that was the only place they could hold him. He was unstoppable."

Not even a bullet could stop Roger Daggitt. He had once been shot three times with a .22 calibre rifle while trying to steal an 8-track tape deck. The owner of the car, a suspected drug dealer by the name of Gord Nakata, interrupted the robbery and fired three bullets into Daggitt, including one that lodged in the back of his neck. It was said that the doctors who treated him thought the muscles in his neck had stopped the bullets and saved his life. Daggitt later wore those bullets on a chain around his neck.

Vic Sharma, an East Ender who became a Clark Parker, was friends with Daggitt. "Roger's mother liked to drink," Sharma says. "I heard that she used to go down to the Marr Hotel pub, across from Oppenheimer Park, and she'd put him and his sister in the trunk of her car, with some holes in the bottom so they could get air. She'd leave them in there with a couple of pepperoni sticks and a twenty-sixer of pop while she'd drink all day—that's why he was a hard guy. Roger wasn't someone you messed with. He became a hard-core killer. No one messed with Roger since he was seventeen."

Born on Remembrance Day in 1953, Daggitt developed an early interest in weightlifting, and as he matured, his size would complement his growing strength. Those who knew him personally insist that Daggitt could be friendly, even funny, but it was his association with the Clark Park gang that would first bring him to the attention of police.

Mac Ryan recalls an early encounter with Daggitt. "Gerry Gavin brought Roger around. They had known each other a long time. We were at a party, hanging out on the fire escape, when they came in. Daggitt leaned out the window and said, 'Hey, what's going on?' He grabbed me by the ankle suddenly and hung me off the balcony, four floors up. I'm screaming and looking down at the ground—I had no idea if he was going to let me go. He was showing off and kidding around, but I wasn't too impressed. There was just something that went wrong with him; he could turn on you."

"Roger was a good guy, but he could be very mean," says Gary Blackburn. "He was big. I think he became one of the strongest guys in Canada. But he wasn't the one you needed to worry about. That was Wayne [Angelucci] or Gerry [Gavin]. Wayne was considered the toughest guy in the East End. When Wayne and Gerry were out together, it was just devastating. And when Roger was with them, they could really be trouble. I wouldn't want to be the one to have crossed them."

Captured playing hooky in the 1970s by legendary street photographer Foncie Pulice: Gerry Gavin (left), Roger Daggitt (centre), and Wayne Angelucci. PHOTO: Foncie Pulice

Born in 1952, Wayne Angelucci grew up around the Trout Lake area and had left school by grade seven. "I wasn't interested in what the difference was between the Pacific or the Atlantic Ocean, or how far away Neptune or Pluto were," he says. "I liked shop class, but I wanted to get out." He would spend his afternoons roaming the streets with other East End kids. "We would hang around the railyards, hopping the trains or putting stuffed sleeping bags on the train tracks to scare the engine drivers." He eventually fell in with the Clark Park scene where he gained notoriety for his considerable skill in climbing the tall trees in the park exceptionally well—a skill that came in handy when police constables unexpectedly showed up to raid the park at night.

As far back as he can remember, Angelucci recalls that the police and the courts had it out for the Clark Park gang. "The cops seemed to target Clark

Park like ... all the crime in the East End came from there. And if you went to court for an assault charge or for fighting, and the [prosecutor] said, 'He's a Clark Park member,' that was it—you'd get sent away just on that basis."

Angelucci first met other Clark Parkers at Ben's Café, an old diner that stood next to the Rio Bowling Alley where he worked as a pinsetter. The café was a focal point for a number of Clark Parkers, in part due to its jukebox filled with the sort of rabble-rousing music that appealed to them, from "Itchycoo Park" by the Small Faces to "I Fought The Law" by the Bobby Fuller Four. "East Enders from all over would come [to Ben's Café]. 'Who's got the stolen car tonight?—Hey, I'm going with you,' it was like that," he says, punctuating his sentences frequently with a laugh as he recalls the good old, bad old days.

Angelucci remembers first meeting Gerry Gavin at Ben's. At age twelve or thirteen, the two of them would head downtown, climb up the telephone poles in the alley behind the Orpheum Theatre, and break into one of the windows at the back of the building to watch movies. Of medium height and somewhat stocky build, Gavin gained a reputation as someone who could take a punch then come back at you twice as hard—a reputation that grew as he got older. "Gerry was solid," Angelucci says. "You know if you got into a fight, he'd stick with you and wouldn't run."

For Gerry Gavin, the die had been cast long before the day he'd invited Mac Ryan to Clark Park when he got out of the JDH. Gavin's family extended back at least two generations in Vancouver's criminal history and were known to police from districts all over the city. Gavin's father and uncle, the Burns brothers, were two downtown rounders who had "run" Granville Street as mid-level organized crime figures in the 1960s. When Gavin was still an infant, his father left the family, and the boy was given his mother's maiden name.

Gerry's mother, Ruth Gavin, rose to become one of East Vancouver's most notorious and well-known heroin dealers. "When I later ended up in jail in Oakalla, all the old hypes [heroin addicts] knew Ruth Gavin," says Bradley Bennett. Ruth dealt heroin directly out of the family home at 1363 East 5th Avenue. "She was from the Hastings Street crowd," adds retired constable Grant MacDonald, who began his policing career on the Hastings Street beat in the mid-1960s. There, he and other beat police had known Ruth to be a prostitute who worked the area. "In those days, Hastings Street was practically the heroin users' capital of Canada. Ruth Gavin was using heroin, but she was also trafficking. Personally, she wasn't unpleasant to deal with, but she'd spawned this wild kid always in trouble and getting arrested. Everybody knew Gerry Gavin."

Even Gerry Gavin's grandmother Lilian had been a part of the family business—she was an old Polish-born bootlegger from prohibition days. "She had a little hideout behind the stool where she sat in their home," says Wayne Angelucci. "She'd hit a spring and a door would open and out would pop a mickey of booze if you wanted to buy one."

"Gerry was the most feared out of all of us," says Gary Blackburn. "He wasn't afraid to do anything. He was the most extreme. You could fuck around with Wayne, you could fuck around with Roger even, but Gerry—I say this with him being a close friend—you had to toe the line. He could be a very dangerous dude."

By the late 1960s, complaints from neighbours about disruptive youths in Clark Park were on the rise. And many local residents began to voice concerns that the area was going downhill fast due to increased burglaries, vandalism, and violence.

"My grandmother used to go to bingo nights on Commercial Drive," Rick Stuart says. "One night she was walking home by the park when I wasn't there. Some guys saw her and were going to steal her purse or mug her. I heard later that one of them recognized my grandmother and said, 'Hey, don't do it—that's Stuart's grandmother,' and she made it home, oblivious to the whole thing." There were at least some neighbours of Clark Park who enjoyed immunity from the gang, even if they didn't realize it.

"If you weren't from there or around the area, you'd get beat up," adds Gary Blackburn. "That's the way it was then. Little kids were safe and protected by us a lot of the time, but if you weren't part of the people at the park and found yourself around there, you'd be in trouble."

Vancouver police began to respond to complaints but with limited success. The very size of the park made it difficult for just a pair of officers to properly respond to an incident. "Nobody could catch you in Clark Park," explains Blackburn. "There were too many exits. They would have to surround the park with practically 100 police cars, and you'd still find your way out. You were safe there."

If the gang members were in the park, they were fairly easy to spot. Many of the Clark Parkers donned red "mack" jackets. Durable, inexpensive, and warm, the mack could be worn as both a shirt and jacket. It became popular in the 1970s, and not only among East Vancouver youth. The jacket had long been worn as work clothing by loggers in the province throughout the 1950s and '60s. When they returned from work outside the city to their family homes in East Vancouver, they left behind hand-me-downs for growing boys to wear, as they could easily and affordably be replaced.

"The red mack jacket was pretty common with all of us," says Bennett. "They made them green and black or red and black, but I had one that was blue, red, and black. So I stood out a little," he says, laughing. "Everybody was always asking me where I got it. Some Main Street guys even tried to steal it off me.

"We used to cut the sleeves off so they were even, and we'd wear our cut-off jean jackets on top," says Mac Ryan. "We looked like quite a force. If you see thirty guys in mack jackets coming down the street, you don't give them too much trouble. We protected our turf. Everybody in Vancouver knew not to come to Clark Park."

Patches with gang logos weren't worn with the jackets, but several Clark Parkers considered designing some. Taking a page from the motorcycle clubs who often had an M.C. abbreviation on their logos, they contemplated making Clark Park S.G. "street gang" patches.

Clark Park would enter its most notorious period in the early 1970s. Petty vandalism, minor theft, and assaults continued, but the reach of the gang extended itself as never before. Soon headline-making civil disorder compounded fears that the chaos that the new gangs brought with them was something for which Vancouver wasn't prepared. No longer dismissing them as teenage ruffians, police prioritized their dealings with the Clark Park gang as a criminal problem they could no longer ignore.

Vancouver Mayor Tom Campbell (here in 1972): "When people take to beating up the police or throwing rocks at them and breaking windows, they're nothing but punks. And it's the punks I'm out to get rid of."
PHOTO: Ralph Bower, *Vancouver Sun*

FIVE: GENERAL ADMISSION

Few figures in the history of Vancouver civic politics are remembered for causing as much political discord as Mayor Tom Campbell. Campbell rose from serving as an alderman in the 1960s to replace Bill Rathie as mayor in 1966, just as the city's counterculture was flowering. But he was not a fat-cat, septuagenarian, pre-war politician distanced from youth by a significant age gap—which might have made his conservative values understandable. Campbell became mayor at the age of just thirty-nine, though this was the era when young hippies distrusted anyone over thirty, and anyone over thirty distrusted those with long hair or a beard. Despite his relative youth, he appeared to unabashedly represent an old-guard, chamber-of-commerce mindset and believed that Vancouver's future would be safe in the hands of local property-development interests. There was no question about his passion or sincerity, but it often seemed to get the better of him; he was not a rousing speaker, and his replies could be marred by a stammer when he was personally criticized over public policy.

Campbell would seemingly spend his final term as mayor—and whatever political capital he had—with an axe to grind. He was repeatedly at odds with not only the city's significant population of young people, but entire neighbourhoods. He attempted to shut down the weekly counterculture newspaper *The Georgia Straight*, championed proposals that would have brought a freeway through Chinatown, backed the proposed demolition of the historic Carnegie Centre building, and supported the construction of a luxury hotel at the entrance to Stanley Park. Campbell lashed out at anyone who failed to support his development plans, labelling them "Maoists, pinkos, left wingers and hamburgers."[27] (Campbell apparently defined a hamburger to mean anyone without a high school education.) He once claimed that any development proposal scuttled by city council would mean a victory for the Communist Party of

27 Michael Kluckner, *Vancouver Remembered* (Vancouver, BC: Whitecap Books, 2006), 87.

Canada.[28] Many regarded him as a publicity hound who would pose for any photo as long as it raised his or what he considered the city's profile. Today, history does not remember Campbell kindly. Generations of civic historians will continue to wince at the photo of the smiling face of Tom "Terrific" sitting in a bulldozer wearing a hardhat, celebrating the demolition of historic buildings including the Lyric Theatre—the original ornate Vancouver Opera House,

Tom Campbell (manning a bulldozer in 1972) once claimed that any city development proposal scuttled by city council would mean a victory for Communism. PHOTO: *Vancouver Sun*

built in 1889—in order to usher in the Pacific Centre mall complex.

In a famous interview with the CBC on the steps of the Vancouver courthouse, Campbell addressed the arrests of hippies who'd been charged with loitering in that same spot. In a lengthy statement delivered in a tone tinged with disgust, he called out barefoot hippies, lazy louts, draft dodgers, and parasites who had come to Vancouver, as well as the youth counterculture as a whole. "We've got a major problem facing the city of Vancouver," he told the CBC. "We've got a 'scum community' who are organized ... These people don't deserve any support. I think the support should go to our good youth, our Boy Scouts, the organizations in town—the church, the decent children ... I'll show you good, decent, clean citizens that need help," he continued. "The majority of

28 "Pinkos—Vancouver Mayor Raps Opposition To Bridge," *Ottawa Citizen*, February 9, 1972, 10.

Vancouver police surveillance photo of a hippie "Be-In" at Stanley Park in the 1970s. PHOTO: Vancouver Police Museum, PO1782

us are decent, hard-working people ... What would happen if our country continued this way? Within the next two generations, there wouldn't be a country. And if these young people do get their way, they will destroy Canada, and from what I hear across the world, they will destroy the world ... The fact that our youth are a part of it, it's decaying and it's rotten."[29]

Today, Campbell is regarded as a somewhat cartoonish figure for his stance against Vancouver hippies and their contribution to the moral decline of Vancouver, but it's easy to forget that many citizens at the time agreed with him. Many—especially older Vancouverites in the late 1960s and early '70s—looked on any bearded or longhaired youths as suspicious dope-fiends, dropouts, or radicals.

While Campbell began his diatribes against the hippies who had infested Vancouver, he would soon shift his target to youth gangs. Police and the public also began to notice that the park gangs weren't just causing trouble around their immediate turf, but had shown up all over the city and become a general threat. "We didn't just hang around the park," admits Bradley Bennett. "We'd go all over the city. But there was no sitting down at a big boardroom table and saying, 'What's our plan tonight? What are were going to do?' We were never

29 CBC Digital Archives, http://www.cbc.ca/archives/entry/vancouver-politicians-averse-to-hippies

that organized." And on many nights, aimless and looking for somewhere to go, the gang could show up anywhere, and often in the most unlikely of places.

One weekend in February 1970, Bennett and several other Clark Parkers attended the annual Variety Club telethon at the Queen Elizabeth Theatre where actor Leonard Nimoy was a celebrity guest host. There were no Trekkies among the gang, nor was there a plan for a daring raid to steal from the cash donation boxes. The twenty-four-hour-long event was simply a way to stay out all night and misbehave.

"We'd all gone down there and got stoned on acid," Bennet recalls. "You can imagine what it's like being in the middle of something like a telethon on LSD. But then we saw these other guys in leather jackets, and we realized there was a bunch of Riley Park gang guys there as well. It's really easy to get confused on acid—you think, 'I think those guys are gonna get us, we should kick their ass first' sort of thing." Seated in the studio audience, Clark Parker Paul Melo got into a dust-up with one of the Riley Park gang members, and a fight broke out in the middle of the broadcast. All of them got kicked out of the theatre, but they laughed like hyenas on the way out the door.

Given their behaviour, it's rare to find anyone who can recall the Clark Parkers being invited guests anywhere. A fight was almost always expected to take place, whether the gang showed up to crash a university frat party or a high school house party at some residence on the west side where the parents were out of town. These were opposite worlds colliding that exploded the moment the gang entered the front door.

They were also rarely welcomed as guests to counterculture events in town. While the hippies might have shared the Clark Parkers' general anti-authoritarianism and interest in getting stoned, peace and love didn't necessarily extend to the gang. "We heard about some party on 4th Avenue near Granville Island. So about two or three carloads of us headed down there," explains Rick Stuart. "Some of our girlfriends were with us too, and we just showed up to enjoy ourselves, have a few pops, and hang out. Well, I guess these hippies didn't like the cut of our jibs—maybe mackinaws weren't the fashion, and the problem was we didn't have tie-died shirts? But sure as shit, some fight starts breaking out and we're throwing guys through windows. It was crazy. Doors were getting ripped off their hinges. We tore that joint up bad, and took off before the police showed up." The hippie Be-Ins taking place in Stanley Park in the late 1960s where hippies played music, blew bubbles, smoked pot, and danced barefoot in the mud, were also a draw for curious Clark Parkers. But when the gatherings turned into political rallies—something that the gang had little interest in—it further differentiated and distanced the greasers from the more socially conscious hippies.

By the beginning of 1970s, the gang's reputation for causing trouble was beginning to make headlines. And the police had noticed that the Clark Parkers had been at a number of notorious city battles. "Punk Gangs Take Over English Bay" was the July 16, 1970, front-page headline of *The Province*, reporting on the week-long Sea Festival. The free annual festival attracted thousands of peaceful crowds to English Bay during the summer for live entertain-

Punk gangs take over English Bay

By PAUL MANNING
Province Staff Reporter

Trouble-seeking hoodlums have taken English Bay away from the West End residents and Vancouver visitors who used to take late night strolls along the beach to cool off on a hot summer's night.

The repeated violence and vandalism of the past few nights is not being created by the neighborhood residents, or by American draft dodgers, or by the thousands of students who wound up in Vancouver during their summer tour of Canada.

The troublemakers have been punks—most of them Canadian and almost all of them residents of Vancouver — pawns of the political activists who stir them up and fade away as soon as the police arrive, according to Mayor Campbell.

They aren't an organized gang or political conspiracy, but rather loosely-knit bands of elder delinquents who've decided that the way to get their follies on a hot summer night is to go down to the beach and throw a few rocks at the cops.

While political activist groups such as the Vancouver Liberation Front and the yippies have been in evidence prior to most of the disturbances, spokesmen for the groups disclaim any part in the aftermath of rioting that has followed the normal nightly meetings on the beaches of English Bay.

Reporters who have covered the disturbances generally support this statement.

Mayor Campbell has tried to quiet talk of vigilante groups of West End residents planning their own patrols to clear the troubled area.

"I have told them the police are doing an excellent job and to leave everything in their hands," said the mayor.

But Campbell said it is unfortunate that the "good kids" in Vancouver are getting a black eye because of the actions of a trouble-making few.

"There are about 200 punks who are making a bad name for the 100,000 good kids in this city," he said.

"When some people take to beating up the police or throwing rocks at them and breaking windows, then they're nothing but punks.

"And it's the punks I'm out to get rid of," said Campbell.

Campbell said his information indicated Wednesday morning's clash between rioters and the police was instigated by the VLF and yippies.

"They (the VLF and yippies) had people hiding behind the baths at English Bay," said Campbell. "They started it by lighting the fires and moving people into the streets by beating drums, and then they faded away when the police arrived."

Campbell said the VLF and yippie people cleared out at the sight of police because "they're too smart to hang around and get picked up."

Continued on Page 13
See POLITICAL

Crowd problems and disorder marred the Vancouver Sea Festival in 1970.
SOURCE: *The Province*

ment as well as the legendary bathtub races. During the 1970 event, however, police had to deal with instances of violence and vandalism—on one evening alone, ten people were injured and thirty arrested—that marred several nights of the event, forcing the cancellation of some of the outdoor street dances, which had become focal points for the disturbances. One night, thirty-six members of the Vancouver police riot squad were dispatched to the festival.

The riots even made the national news; the *Montreal Gazette* reported that on multiple evenings, after the evening program ended and crowds were dispersing, fights broke out with "people gathered at English Bay beach, who were flooding nearby streets, smashing windows, setting fire to garbage cans, rocking passing transit buses and private automobiles, and pelting them with rocks."[30]

Meanwhile, *The Province* assured its readers that the disorder was "not being created by the neighbourhood residents, or by American draft dodgers, or the thousands of students who wound up in Vancouver during their summer tour of Canada." Instead, "the troublemakers have been punks—most of them Canadian

30 "Youths in Vancouver Protest Festival Ban," *Montreal Gazette*, July 16, 1970, 21.

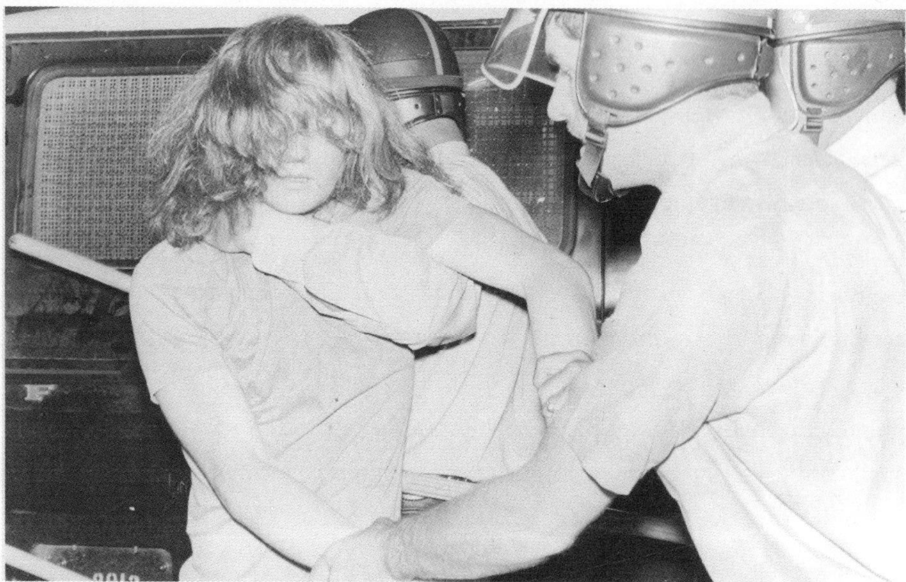

VPD surveillance photographers captured photos of the Gastown rioters as they were arrested, August 7, 1971.
PHOTO: Vancouver Police Museum, P00281

and almost all of them residents of Vancouver ... They aren't an organized gang or political conspiracy, but rather loosely knit bands of elder delinquents who've decided the only way to get their jollies on a hot summer night is to go down to the beach and throw a few rocks at the cops."[31]

Mayor Tom Campbell was no less candid in his opinion: "There are about 200 punks who are making a bad name for the 100,000 good kids in this city. When some people take to beating up the police, or throwing rocks at them and breaking windows, they're nothing but punks. And it's the punks I'm out to get rid of," he said.[32]

Vancouver's counterculture didn't entirely escape blame for the trouble—in fact, everyone from youth gangs to hippies to a local Marxist-Leninist group called the Vancouver Liberation Front, whom the police had surveilled, were named as culprits. Mouse Williamson admits that his gang was also involved in the Sea Festival disruptions. "One of those nights [in English Bay] started with us, [when] one of our guys and a bunch of West End guys got into a fight, and we all jumped in—it turned into a real battle royal. The mounted police came in on their horses in the middle of it."

31 "Punk Gangs Take Over English Bay," *The Province*, July 16, 1970, 1.
32 Ibid.

Gastown was the site of the next battle a year later. Mayor Campbell had pointed the finger at the area as the "soft drug capital of Canada"[33] and aggressively promoted a cleanup. Gastown was then unlike the strip of upscale bars, eateries, and shops it is today. In 1971 the district was just beginning to undergo a period of renewal after years as a semi-industrial area of warehouses; old buildings were being renovated, boutiques were opening, and the area was taking on life again. A year earlier, the drinking age had been lowered from twenty-one to nineteen in BC, and Gastown became a more attractive haunt for young people, especially university students and hippies from the Kitsilano neighbourhood who socialized in the local beer parlours or worked in Gastown during the day. But in 1971, arrests for possession and trafficking of marijuana and hash were suddenly outnumbering arrests for heroin, and so Gastown came under increasing scrutiny from Vancouver police.[34]

On August 7, 1971, after weeks of police crackdowns—named Operation Dustpan—on marijuana dealing and smoking in Gastown, a peaceful protest was organized by two writers from *The Georgia Straight*. The city considered it a demonstration for the legalization of marijuana. The protest took on a circus-like atmosphere as 2,000 hippies, squatters, stoners, and curiosity-seeking regular citizens of all ages descended on Water Street and the surrounding avenues. "We went down for the smoke-in," recalls Mac Ryan, who was there along with Rick Stuart and Albert Hill. "There were people giving away joints, and [we saw] a guy with a massive joint a few feet long. It was a good atmosphere; everybody was relaxed and having a good time."

Riot squad police on horseback held back at first. But the crowd was vocal as cheers of "Fuck Campbell! Fuck Campbell" were hoarsely bellowed in an insistent rhythm. Perhaps sensing that the mood of the crowd was shifting, Ryan and Hill climbed up to a balcony ledge above the door of the Hotel Europe at Powell and Carrall streets where they began to yell, "We're taking over. Clark Park's in charge! Clark Park! Clark Park!," cheering and hollering with the enthusiasm of a state delegation waving their banners on the floor of a political convention. "All the hippies were clapping for us," Ryan recalls. "I felt like a bit of a celebrity."

33 Larry Campbell, Dominque Clément, and Gregory S. Keale, eds., *Debating Dissent: Canada and the Sixties* (Toronto, ON: University of Toronto Press, 2012), 122.
34 Joe Swan, *A Century of Service: The Vancouver Police 1886–1986* (Vancouver, BC: Vancouver Police Historical Society and Centennial Museum, 1986), 112.

Bradley Bennett, Mark Owens, and Dennis Magnus, 1970s.
PHOTO: Courtesy of Bradley Bennett

Minutes later, when the glass window of a storefront was shattered, the police ordered everyone to leave the street within two minutes. When the order was ignored (or perhaps not even heard above the din of the crowd), police officials ordered four mounted officers to disperse the throng, followed by police in riot gear, which caused the demonstration to explode. The resulting chaos left Water Street blood-spattered and full of broken glass. Twelve citizens were hospitalized, seventy-nine arrested, and thirty-eight people were charged with various offences.[35] The delegation from Clark Park managed to escape amid all the confusion.

Not in attendance that evening was Bradley Bennett. "I was in juvie that night," he explains. "They arrested a lot of people that night—they ran out of cells and woke us up at two in the morning to put another guy in each of our rooms."

Later, the inquiry into the riot would rule that the police overreacted against the protest, though this was quietly disputed for years by many of the members of the police department who were there that night. Either way, the VPD would make sure that the next time the police riot squad was deployed, they would be better prepared.

Mark Owens was born in 1954 and raised in East Vancouver. He had known Mac Ryan from around the neighbourhood, but didn't come into con-

35 Michael Barnholden, *Reading the Riot Act: A Brief History of Riots in Vancouver* (Vancouver, BC: Anvil Press, 2005), 92.

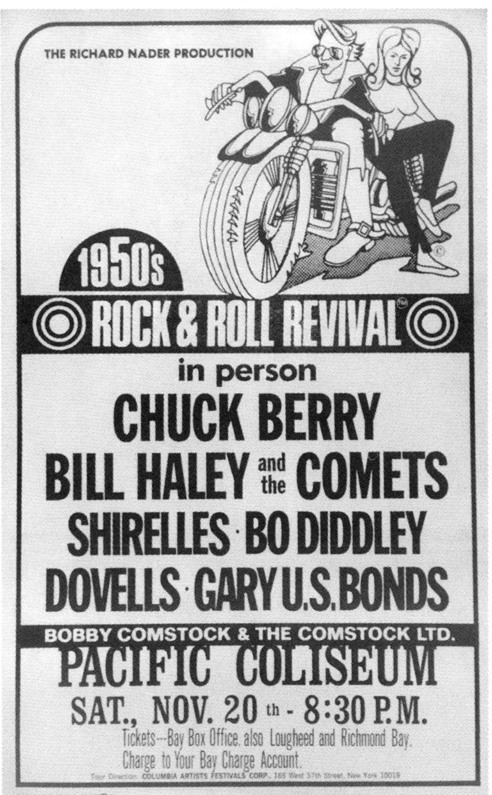

The Rock and Roll Revival at the Pacific Coliseum in 1971 descended into chaos before Chuck Berry or Bill Haley even took the stage.
PHOTO: Courtesy of Neptoon Records

tact with other members of the Clark Park gang until 1968, after he'd served time in Brannen Lake jail. Upon release, he found himself drafted into the scene at Clark Park. "There were a lot of gang fights with bats," Owen recalls. "Sometimes the fights were over girls. But my cousin hung around Riley Park, so it was always a little weird for me, as I knew those Riley Park gang guys too."

"Along with Roger and Gerry, Mark was a real animal, a wild guy back then," says Bradley Bennett. "We once got into a fight over a girl, and he hit me pretty badly by swinging a heavy belt buckle against my head. I needed to get stitches, but he came with me to the hospital and we made up afterward and became friends."

A talented musician, Owens was later a drummer in a local rock band, Circus Mind. Some friends thought he even bore a resemblance to Chuck Berry, and when Berry himself came to town, Owens and a number of other Clark Parkers, including Wayne Angelucci, Gerry Gavin, Mouse Williamson, and Gary Blackburn, all decided to go to the concert.

"It's a real live Rock and Roll Revival on Saturday November 20, 8:30 p.m. at the Pacific Coliseum!" announced legendary Vancouver radio DJ Red Robinson in an advertisement that aired in the weeks prior to the concert, which was to feature not only Berry but an all-star lineup including Bill Haley and the Comets, the Shirelles, Bo Diddley, the Dovells, and Gary U.S. Bonds. On the day of the show, an audience of an estimated 11,000 entered the Coliseum without incident.

Doug MacNichol, then just sixteen years old, was a student from Vancouver Technical Secondary School. "It wasn't like today where there are pat-downs or they search you to see if you're bringing in alcohol. There was none of that. It was pretty loose that way," he says. The lack of strict security at the entrances meant many people easily smuggled in their own bottles of alcohol. But the concert itself started well. The sounds of doo-wop and classic rock 'n' roll almost time-warped the Coliseum back to the late 1950s and early '60s when the groups performing were first popular. Both the initial opening acts—Bonds and the Dovells—were well received.

Perhaps too well. As the concert had been sold with reserved seating, eager rock 'n' roll fans, already feeling the Old Style pilsner in their veins, left their seats to dance in the open area in front of the stage. The mood of the crowd was not yet problematic. But just before Bo Diddley's set, the first signs of trouble appeared when an emcee stepped onto the stage to announce over the PA that the fire marshal would cancel the show if the floor in front of the stage wasn't cleared, and asked that people return to their seats. Some but not all of the audience moved away from the area when Diddley kicked off his set, leaving a crowd up front that wasn't particularly interested in being told what to do.

"They were really enthusiastic," Diddley would say the following day in an interview with the *Vancouver Sun*. "But then the stage started wobbling, and I began to get kind of worried, so I stopped and asked for the lights to be put on. There were guys down in front of me pulling apart the stage, while others were shouting for the show to go on. I said to myself, 'This thing is going to go. It's time I got my hat.'"[36] Cutting short his set, Diddley left the stage. The approximately 400 audience members in front had now stopped dancing, and scuffles began to break out. The mood of the audience as a whole was becoming increasingly edgy and aggressive.

Again, an emcee came out to admonish the crowd to move back, and announced a fifteen-minute break. Hundreds of audience members began to head for the exits or move to the concourse to inquire about refunds. Those who remained in the audience thought the show would continue, but it would not. As a precaution, the performers who were still scheduled to play were ushered to a bus parked behind the Coliseum and given the chance to depart before the

36 "Rampaging Coliseum Crowd Sends Rock Stars Fleeing," *Vancouver Sun*, November 21, 1971, 2.

cancellation was officially announced to the crowd. Once the announcement was made, rumours quickly circulated that Berry was never in the building to begin with, and the fact that the headliner of the show wasn't going to play only angered those in the audience even further.

Describing the incident, a *Vancouver Sun* reporter wrote: "When a man came to the microphone to tell the crowd that Chuck Berry would not perform because of harassment by the audience, some in the crowd got unruly." The music reviewer from *The Georgia Straight*, meanwhile, reported on the incident with far more colour and period slang: "[The emcee], one of the most bad vibing, bullshit ridden twits I have ever come across ... a natty little capitalist in a beige sports jacket, in no uncertain terms told the crowd, 'This is my show, this is my stage, and you're fucking it up!'" The reporter went on to say that "there was a feeling of inevitable violence ... and the fatal words were finally uttered from the stage, 'There are a bunch of cops out back and if you don't leave they'll come and move you out.'"[37]

There were about twenty members of the Clark Park gang in the audience. They decided that it was time for them to make their mark. "All we had heard was that Chuck Berry refused to go on because we were sitting too close to the stage," says Wayne Angelucci. "So we got up on stage, people started throwing bottles, and the whole place went nuts." As a joke, Angelucci picked up one of the band's guitars that had been left there and pretended to play it. Another member of the audience followed his lead and started to mimic playing the piano. Stagehands, too afraid to step on stage while bottles were being thrown, abandoned their positions in the wings and took cover.

The stage was now being torn apart by angry people below it, and several East Enders followed Angelucci's lead, grabbing musical instruments and pretending to play them. The Coliseum dissolved into pandemonium as more people on the floor, as well as those in the stands, suddenly starting to throw the beer bottles they'd snuck into the concert. "I looked up and saw all these bottles coming [at me], so I hid behind the tower of PA speakers," remembers Angelucci. "They struck the tower so hard, the speakers moved back."

Rob Thacker, another Clark Parker on the stage, was thrown off by a stagehand. He was cut in the chest by shards of glass on the floor at the same moment that someone else threw a bottle at Angelucci and struck him squarely in the

37 Rick McGrath, "Rock and Roll Rip-off," *The Georgia Straight*, November 25, 1971, 5, 11.

head. "When we saw that, we all jumped up on stage and started kicking the shit out of the guy who threw it," recalls Mouse Williamson. "But we were getting hit by the bottles that people were throwing onto the stage, so we threw some equipment—like microphones and anything else that wasn't bolted down—out into the crowd." Staggering for a moment after the bottle smashed into his head, Angelucci looked up as the blood flowed freely from the cut. "There were so many bottles flying in the air, they looked like swarm of locusts or birds passing overhead or something, so I jumped back down."

Sixteen-year-old Doug MacNichol was still on the floor watching the chaos ensue. "All hell broke loose," he recalls. "It seemed like there were no cops in the building or any presence of authority. It was the strangest thing. Even the ushers in the Coliseum must have realized that it was now going to be the Wild West, and they got out of there as well. Bottles were being thrown, not just on the floor where I was, but from the upper seats as well. A woman standing near me got hit in the head with a bottle."

Those being hit with bottles crawled over seats, breaking the backs of chairs to get out of the crowd and to safety. People yelled and shoved each other as they ran to the exits. The few brave stagehands who hadn't abandoned the stage were desperately trying to move expensive musical instruments or amplifiers that still sat on stage and hadn't been stolen. ("Word had it that one of the guitars ended up in the woodworking shop at Vancouver Technical [school] for 'repairs,'" notes MacNichol.)

A previously unseen sense of Good Samaritanism suddenly came over Angelucci and Williamson who came to the aid of a stagehand rolling a piano to safety, only to look at each other and wonder why they were helping. They both let go of the piano, which rolled and pinned the stagehand against the wall while the Clark Parkers returned to the fighting.

A large mobile condiment truck on the concourse near the hot dog stand was pushed down a flight of stairs. And whether because they felt the concert had been a rip-off or they felt the joy of drunkenly running amok and smashing anything in the Coliseum they could, audience members began to trash the restrooms and shatter the Plexiglas panels that were part of the ice rink. Meanwhile, a CBC TV news cameraman arrived, dispatched to cover the chaos as soon as word had reached the newsroom over the police scanners that a riot was breaking out inside the Coliseum.

Mark Owens was concerned about how to escape. "I had warrants out on me, so I thought I better get the hell out of there, but police were suddenly at all the exits," he says. "I finally made it out, and the last thing I saw was Angelucci still on stage with a bloodied towel on his head." The rest of the Clark Park gang fled the building, evading police in the confusion. It was midnight before stoned concert stragglers who had passed out in the aisles and ushers who had hidden in offices for safety were finally cleared from the building.

The next day, CBC television's evening news would begin its broadcast with the Coliseum incident as their lead story: "The future of rock concerts at the PNE grounds has been left in doubt by the outbreak of destruction last night at the Pacific Coliseum. Part of a crowd of 11,000 began throwing bottles and smashing musical equipment during a show billed as a rock and roll revival."[38] Noting that an undetermined number of injuries and arrests had been made, CBC's reporter continued: "Broken bottles and glass were everywhere, and estimates of the damage amounts to $20,000," adding lastly that, "Mayor Campbell has remarked that he personally favours a ban on further rock concerts."

The broadcast didn't include all of the film footage caught by the CBC cameraman from the night before. Vivid images of the battle would show dozens of police who had arrived around the perimeter of the Coliseum concourse surveying rows of smashed floor seats, shattered Plexiglas boards, washroom mirrors and sinks, and the broken glass doors of the Coliseum. One shot showed audience members trying to assist stagehands dragging gear and equipment to safety.

However, of all the images televised to tens of thousands of homes across the Lower Mainland during that evening's newscast, one scene stood out: three men on stage hollering taunts and violently launching bottles back into the audience. They were Wayne Angelucci, Mouse Williamson, and Gerry Gavin. The Clark Parkers had arrived.

38 CBC Television News, Untitled film strip, dated November 21, 1971. (Vancouver, BC: CBC Vancouver Archives).

A demonstration at the opening of the Georgia Viaduct in January 1972.
PHOTO: George Diack, *Vancouver Sun*

Demonstrators kicked and spat at the windows and even jumped on the hood of the car of Mayor Tom Campbell's motorcade as it passed in January 1972.
PHOTO: Ross Kenward, *The Province*

SIX: EXILE ON RENFREW STREET

On a cold Sunday in January of 1972, Mayor Tom Campbell celebrated the opening of the Georgia Viaduct by driving across it in a gleaming black limousine. The newly constructed overpass had been one of the most controversial of the proposals that Campbell championed during his tenure as mayor. Its construction raised consternation from the start; it was to be the first phase of a new highway through the city that when completed would result in the partial destruction of the East Vancouver areas of Chinatown, Gastown, and Strathcona.

Escorting the limousine were members of the Vancouver police motorcycle squad, and media were on hand to record the motorcade. The mayor's vehicle approached the western end of the viaduct to find a crowd of demonstrators. The car came to a halt for a moment while police did their best to attempt some measure of crowd control. Demonstrators kicked the limousine, spat at the windows, and even jumped on the hood before the car surged forward and passed through.

Vancouver historian Michael Kluckner, who was present that day as one of the demonstrators in the crowd, wrote in his book *Vancouver Remembered*: "Eventually the motorcade made it through. That night all the newscasts decried the protest as the work of thugs, agitators and troublemakers."[39] The confrontation on the viaduct might have served as a parable for the rest of 1972—city hall and the police, with the general public on their side, were not going to let the lunatics take over the asylum.

This would be remembered as a violent year in police quarters: homicides in Vancouver reached an all-time high of twenty-three, and there was an increase in the number of people arrested for firearms use. A wave of heavily armed bank holdups hit the city, and prostitution was becoming a more serious issue, with a total of 435 charges laid, including some against male prostitutes. Drugs were still an issue, with 222 people charged with trafficking heroin and 348

39 Kluckner, *Vancouver Remembered*, 85.

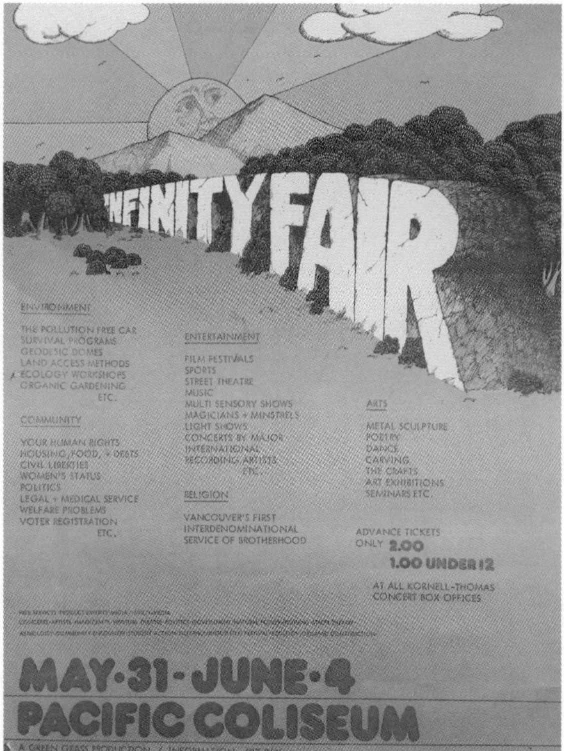

At the Infinity Fair at the Pacific National Exhibition, some exhibitors illicitly sold marijuana and hash to concertgoers.
SOURCE: Courtesy of Neptoon Records

arrested for "soft-drug" use, which included marijuana and LSD.[40]

In April 1972, the Rolling Stones would stun local rock music fans by announcing that their *Exile on Main Street* tour would begin in Vancouver with a concert at the Pacific Coliseum on June 3. By '72, with the Beatles disbanded, the Stones had the pinnacle of rock 'n' roll all to themselves—and they could live up to their designation as "the world's greatest rock 'n' roll band."

The announcement nearly overshadowed the city itself. Vancouver was then a smaller and less internationally prominent place than it is now, and the Pacific Coliseum was hardly Madison Square Garden or Shea Stadium. The fact that a world-renowned rock group like the Rolling Stones would pick a hockey arena on the western edge of Canada to kick off their tour was wholly unexpected. The band hadn't played live in North America for three years, and Vancouver would be their first show since the infamous 1969 concert at Altamont, California, where an audience member had been stabbed to death by Hells Angels acting as concert "security." The band were already locally considered mad, bad, and dangerous to know from their previous appearance in Vancouver in 1966, when police interrupted their set in an attempt to control the unruly audience. In the lingering wake of the previous year's Gastown riot and the chaos at the Rock and Roll Revival just months earlier, civic anxiety about the coming Stones concert was quick to build.

40 Swan, *A Century of Service*, 114.

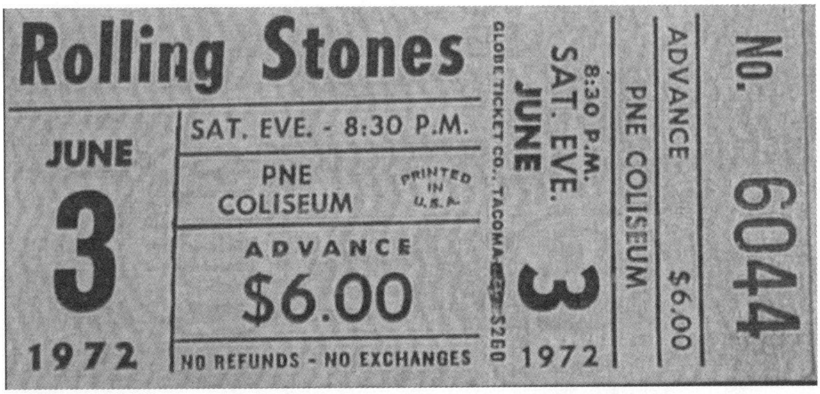

Many concertgoers complained that tickets for the 1972 Rolling Stones concert in Vancouver were exorbitantly priced.
SOURCE: Courtesy of Vince Ricci

"After the Gastown riot, it felt like there had been months of total silence," recalls East Ender Al Walker. "I had about ten friends whose older brothers had their heads bashed in at Gastown. So it felt like everybody was laying low—nobody was hanging out. Even the park scene was really quiet. So when the Stones concert was announced—that was a big event in itself, the first big event in town for months—a lot of people talked about it almost like it was a dare: 'Are you going to go?'"

Fourteen-year-old Nicholas Jones of North Vancouver decided that nothing was going to keep him away. When the tickets went on sale about a month before the show, Jones and his friends camped out overnight at the Empire Stadium box office, where tickets were being sold, to be as close to the front of the line as possible. The ticket price was exorbitantly higher than the then-going rate for a rock concert ticket— six dollars, a full dollar and fifty cents more than the best seats at the Rock and Roll revival. "I don't think anybody believed that the Rolling Stones were really going to be opening the tour here," says Jones. "In those days, you never even got to see them on TV. The only chance to see them was live. It was a huge deal that they were coming to Vancouver, much less starting their tour here."

There were others who were excited about the show for different reasons. In January, a group of political activists made up of disgruntled *Georgia Straight* writers made news when they founded an offshoot of the newspaper called *The Georgia Grape*. Some of those associated with *The Grape* were also involved with an East Vancouver Marxist-Leninist gang called the Youngbloods. When the concert was announced, the Youngbloods, impressed with the growing reputation of the Clark Park gang after the havoc they caused at the Rock and Roll Revival, decided to try and ally them to their own cause. With the promise of a few free cases of beer, the Clark Park gang was invited to the Youngbloods' headquarters at a residential home on Templeton Street in East Vancouver.

Mouse Williamson remembers the meeting. "There was an older guy named Alex who was some kind of communist or anarchist involved with *The Grape* in some way," he says. "He'd photographed a few of us for the newspaper, holding our fists up in the air in solidarity. He and a couple of his friends tried to insinuate themselves into our gang and get us all riled up, but we had no idea what he was talking about. He wanted the Clark Parkers to help them as muscle. He kept going on about 'power to the people,' and was big on 'liberation'—we didn't even know what the fucking word meant. We didn't give a shit about politics."

"They had all these smoke bombs, and they wanted to cause a distraction," remembers Mac Ryan, who was also present at the meeting. "They had a big battle plan: When the doors opened, we're going to toss [the bombs] and then [others] were going to ... crash the gates. We thought, 'What the fuck—what are these guys on about?'"

Williamson, Ryan, and the other gang members on hand didn't like the Youngbloods' style. The political agenda was foreign to them, and the Clark Parkers didn't want to invite that much heat on themselves. Nevertheless, they let the reciting of manifestos and political speeches go on until the free beer and weed had run out, then made their excuses and left. Mac Ryan was particularly unimpressed. "They wanted us to break into the concert, but we realized later they had a separate agenda that wasn't to get into the show for free—they just wanted us to fight the cops."

When the day of the concert arrived, Stevie Wonder—who was opening for the Rolling Stones—decided to do some shopping in Vancouver. He visited an expensive clothing store that sold the kind of full-length mink coats considered chic in the early '70s. As Wonder and his handler tried on some coats, they were profiled as shoplifters by store security who failed to recognize the musician. The embarrassed store manager apologized, and though the outcome of the incident is unknown, one might imagine Wonder being offered the coats not only with an apology but a considerable discount.

While Stevie Wonder was downtown trying on mink coats, in Clark Park Gary Blackburn was also being profiled as he sat on the grass relaxing and chatting with a friend before heading to the Coliseum. Unlike Wonder, however, Blackburn would receive neither an apology nor a discount.

"My friend asked me to watch his coat. So I put it underneath me and sat on it," Blackburn says. "I knew he sold drugs, but I didn't think anything of holding his coat. Well, about five minutes after he left, these two cops came right up to me in the park like they'd been watching me and asked if the coat was mine. I said, 'Excuse me?' And they asked again, 'Is that your jacket?' I told them it wasn't mine. They went right through the pockets and pulled out this little tin, the kind cough lozenges are sold in. They opened it up, and inside was a bunch of hash, some MDA, and a syringe—the works. I didn't know anything was in there, and again I told them it wasn't mine, but I wasn't going to say whose it was, so they told me I was under arrest."

The concert was just hours away, and Blackburn couldn't believe his bad luck. He insisted to the police that the jacket wasn't his, and that he had plans to go to the Rolling Stones concert. The police unexpectedly assured him that they simply had to take him down to the station and book him; he'd be released in time to attend the show.

Feeling more optimistic about his situation despite the arrest, Blackburn was taken to the Main Street police station. But when he arrived at the booking desk, the deal had changed and he was told that he could expect to spend the night in jail. "I said that the officer who picked me up had promised to let me go after they booked me, and the guy just laughed and shook his head, saying, 'It's not up to them.' So I got taken upstairs to the jail cells. I couldn't believe it."

While Blackburn was being booked at the station around three in the afternoon, Rolling Stones fans had begun to show up outside the Coliseum plaza. John Armstrong, a fifteen-year-old student from the suburbs in White Rock who later became known as the Modernettes' lead singer Buck Cherry, had taken the hour-long bus ride into Vancouver to attend the show. "I was beside myself," he says. "This might have been the first or second concert I'd ever been to. The Stones were gods then, and I was just a huge fan. I had two tickets, and I wanted to take a girl in the hope I got laid, but my cousin Dennis had come

By dusk, crowds outside the Pacific Coliseum were beginning to get unruly, and the VPD riot squad prepared for the worst—they'd been tipped that the Clark Park gang was going to crash the concert.
PHOTO: *The Grape*, June 7–13, 1972

to visit from out of town, and my Mom told me, 'If you don't take your cousin, you're not going at all.' The show wasn't even a big deal to him," he says. With his cousin Dennis in tow, Armstrong arrived to see a curious scene in front of the Coliseum. "White Rock was kind of a hippie haven of people back then," he says. "They smoked clay pipes, made dream catchers, and looked like they'd stepped out of a Tolkien novel. So I'd seen hippies before. But the hippies at the Stones' show that day looked really ill and dirty, like they'd all discovered red wine and speed." Armstrong and his cousin, eager to get in line, walked past these unhealthy-looking hippies, and though he noticed a few police officers hanging about, there wasn't a large police presence or any sense of menace in the crowd. There was certainly nothing that gave him any indication of what would transpire later.

From the opposite end of the city, sixteen-year-old Nick Jones had also arrived early from North Vancouver with his friends. As they entered the Coliseum, they encountered the Infinity Fair—a week-long, youth-related crafts fair, now part of the pre-show event inside the arena. There, vendors were selling all manner of tie-dyed fabrics and incense, and booths featuring Hare Krishnas and alternative press publishers sold or gave away their literature. "Those vendors were also selling lots of weed on the sly too," Jones recalls. "I was excited that we were going to see the Rolling Stones, but we were pretty baked by the time the show started." This residual effect hit not only Jones and friends but apparently much of the rest of the audience as well. Sitting in front of Jeani Read, then *The Province* music critic, Jones noticed that she had passed out. "She wrote a bad review of the show in the newspaper the next day, and we always wondered how she wrote it when she wasn't even awake for the show."

Bradley Bennett was there too, and he wanted to make sure he wasn't going to miss a thing—especially after having missed the Rock and Roll Revival. But while thousands of dutiful Rolling Stones fans had lined up overnight a month earlier to purchase tickets, Bennett, along with Clark Park member Paul Melo, showed up at eight p.m. with an altogether different strategy. "Our plan was to find somebody who was scalping tickets, beat him up, and just steal his tickets," he states candidly. Although it was a sold-out show, there were a surprising amount of scalpers at various corners of the plaza, holding tickets going for upwards of twenty dollars apiece.

"We found a scalper who was a hippie, but he wanted to do the deal by some bushes because there was a lot of security walking around. Melo was fucking with him, trying to negotiate a lower price, and I said the price was too high considering the show had already started." As the scalper got impatient and increasingly frustrated at haggling over the price, he rudely told them that he was going to take his business elsewhere, and pushed past them. Melo threw him to the ground and kicked him in the stomach, and Bennett seized the tickets right out of his hand. Leaving the scalper curled up on the ground groaning in pain, they were off to see the show.

"Then we're in the lineup and Melo is in front of me. He shows his ticket and gets through the gate. Then I hear somebody yell, 'Wait! Wait!' It turns out the scalper we'd beaten up was selling fake tickets, so this big security guard grabbed me by the back of the neck and my ass and tossed me out. Melo was already through the turnstiles and into the Coliseum, but I got kicked out before I got in."

By nine p.m., when Stevie Wonder's opening set had ended, there were still some 2,000 people outside the Coliseum. A number of Clark Parkers, including Mouse Williamson, had not made it in either. "Usually at concerts, we'd get one guy to go in who had a ticket, he'd find an exit door to open, and fifty of us would rush in," he says. "Or we'd just rush the turnstiles and jump over them."

Keith Richards and Mick Jagger on stage at the Pacific Coliseum on June 3, 1972.
PHOTO: Dan Scott, *Vancouver Sun*

But Williamson and the other Clark Parkers were outnumbered by the fans crowding the doors, along with hundreds more would-be gate-crashers, curiosity seekers, those left out due to counterfeit tickets, and others who just wanted to get close enough to an open door to hear the music.

While Williamson had spent much of the afternoon drinking heavily, Kurt Langmann, an eighteen-year-old from Langley, had driven into town with friends to see if he could purchase a scalped ticket. He quickly realized that it was a lost cause when he saw the hundreds of people shut out of the arena. "It was starting to get ugly. Some were inciting us to just try to rush the gates and crash our way in."

As the mood of the crowd began to change, and with nightfall setting in, police moved uniformed officers to the nearby Pacific Showmart building behind the Coliseum where, unbeknownst to concertgoers, they'd set up a command centre with helmets, shields, and batons at the ready. What had been a low-key police presence overseeing basic crowd control earlier in the day now quickly redeployed on the plaza in increased numbers—and full riot squad gear. The police had even invited members of the press to attend. It was almost as if they had been tipped off that a riot was going to happen from the beginning.

As fans who were legitimate ticket holders were still entering the Coliseum, someone on the plaza threw what appeared to be a home-made smoke-bomb, followed by a bottle that struck one of the glass entrance doors. "Suddenly there were rocks flying," wrote Kurt Langmann in a 2011 article for the *Aldergrove Star* newspaper. "This was our cue to get out of Dodge, or Vancouver to be more accurate ... We were all country kids, used to working on the farms, and considered ourselves 'jocks' who liked to work out at the boxing club ... We had teen bravado, were full of testosterone, and afraid of no one. However, this was no 'sport' unfolding before our eyes, this was pure insanity."[41]

Eighteen-year-old Sandi Barr had also hoped to find scalped tickets. She and her boyfriend were on the plaza when the chaos began. "We saw two drunk guys pick up another guy who was loaded and start to use him to batter the glass door head-first," she says. "The guy was laughing as they rammed his head against it. I was shocked. I hadn't seen anything like this. Then I felt something whiz past my right ear. I looked to the ground and saw that it was a big boulder somebody had thrown. I said, 'That's it. Let's get out of here.'"

Constable Grant MacDonald, who had been involved in the "Operation Dustpan" cleanup of Gastown, was off-duty on the night of the Gastown riot, but found himself right in the middle of this one. (He told me that he didn't even like the Rolling Stones; Frank Sinatra and Tony Bennett were more his musical cup of tea.) MacDonald had been on the scene since earlier in the day and noticed the mood of the crowd getting worse, especially as the sun went down. He was among the first officers in the riot line, as the crowd began to taunt police and the first bottles were thrown. "You could see our bosses going through this new manual about when we could engage," he says. "You have to understand that the department had just gone through the Gastown riot and in the wake of the inquiry afterwards, they laid out rules that measured the levels of progression of crowd violence that police could respond to. So we were held back for what seemed like an hour, even when the bottles started flying."

41 Kurt Langmann, "You Sense That a Riot Is Brewing? Know When It's Time to Leave," *Aldergrove Star*, June 21, 2011. http://www.aldergrovestar.com/opinion/124322068.html

As author Michael Barnholden notes in his book *Reading the Riot Act*, Vancouver has a "rich history of rioting," from anti-Asian riots in the early 1900s to labour riots in the '30s to sports-event related riots in more recent years. Vancouverites love to riot in good weather—nearly all of the riots have taken place during the city's pleasant and mostly rain-free months of May to September. But not all riots are demonstrations of class war. The Rolling Stones riot in Vancouver is given brief attention by Barnholden, and the Rock and Roll Revival melee is not mentioned at all. On that warm night outside the Coliseum, a heady brew of alcohol, mob mentality, anti-police sentiment, and male machismo were dangerously confined. It was a golden age of casual violence, when the idea of getting drunk and into a fight was an average and perfectly acceptable activity for a Saturday night. And never has a Vancouver riot had such a fitting soundtrack.

The Out to Lunch Bunch (c. 1970s) helped with security at the Rock and Roll Revival concert. PHOTO: Courtesy of Jesse Longbear

While chaos began to erupt outside the Coliseum, inside the Rolling Stones kicked their set off with "Brown Sugar." The concert went on to feature what would be the first live performance of *Exile on Main Street* songs like "Tumbling Dice," a Rolling Stones classic, and was also apparently the only time "Ventilator Blues" has been performed live by the band.

Mick Jagger, wearing a white jumpsuit and scarf, clapped and danced back and forth across the stage. Much of the press reviews focused on him alone. The *Vancouver Sun* reviewer noted that "Jagger is a bolt of lightning on stage, lightning that never dies, his presence is overwhelming, carrying the people away into fantasies which went unexpressed at the concert but still no doubt laying there in the mind, exciting them to visions the very opposite of psychedelic," and claimed that the performance "shook the foundations of Rock music."[42]

While bootlegs of the concert reveal that it wasn't the tightest performance by the band, few who were there cared, especially those on the floor of the arena who could watch the Stones up close in the Coliseum, then a new building, which opened only four years earlier in 1968.

"I remember thinking the show was great," says John Armstrong. "Stevie Wonder's set was probably really good, but all I wanted to see was the Stones. Had Jesus walked out on stage playing a kazoo, I wouldn't have noticed or cared. I just remember how fucking cool both Mick and Keith [Richards] looked on stage."

While the Stones launched into "Rocks Off" inside the Coliseum, the thumping rhythm could be heard outside, where Bradley Bennett—now locked out of the concert—found himself in a group of fifty or sixty people charging the doors in an attempt to break in. "I was running and everybody was yelling and screaming and charging against one of the doors, when all of a sudden some guy arm-barred me in the head and loosened up my teeth. I was flat on the ground seeing stars when somebody picked me up, walked me to the street corner, told me I was in rough shape and ought to head home."

As Mick Jagger strutted like a rooster on the Coliseum stage, and Keith Richards and the band rocked behind him, some Clark Parkers were doing their best to storm the ramparts. Mac Ryan had been in another crowd running the gates and managed to break through successfully. "We went charging in, and a few of us made it through the doors. But what those guys from *The Grape* hadn't told us the night we met with them was that the Out to Lunch Bunch would be there that night."

A self-styled bunch of cowboy roustabouts from Kitsilano on the west

42 Jamie Craig, "Stoned Young Bask in Music of the Stones," *Vancouver Sun*, June 4, 1972.

At the height of the chaos in 1972, the riot squad pushed the crowd back to Renfrew Street. PHOTO: Dan Scott, *Vancouver Sun*

side, the Out to Lunch Bunch had been a kind of gang unto themselves. They were comprised of a loose affiliation of would-be ranchers, and men who had worked as horse wranglers on local film and TV productions (such as Robert Altman's *McCabe and Mrs. Miller,* shot in Greater Vancouver two years earlier). Some of them picked up additional work as security guards for local concerts; the two-fisted crew could be depended on for their size and strength. Despite a strong appetite for marijuana and some alleged dealing of it, they disdained hippie fashions and looked more like they'd just come from an East Texas ranch than a Stanley Park Be-In. "They were huge guys. They just overwhelmed us and gave us a bit of a beating," Ryan says of the fight that broke out. "We started to run out of there and then the cops came in behind us with the riot squad, so we got caught between the Out to Lunch Bunch and the police. All hell broke loose," he recalls, shaking his head.

As Ryan found himself between the cops and a hard place, out on the plaza, Mouse Williamson, who had been drinking most of the day, now found himself in the middle of the crowd when the riot began. "That's when people stared throwing the Molotov cocktails. It wasn't any of the Clark Park guys,

Rioting East Enders initially threw rocks and pieces of fencing at police before they began to toss Molotov cocktails.
PHOTO: Dan Scott, *Vancouver Sun*

and I don't know if those people were connected to *The Grape*. Just then, a cop came up on horseback, grabbed me by the hair, and lifted me off the ground." Williamson broke free, but as he did, the bottle of wine he'd been drinking broke, cutting his fingers. Blood dripping from his hand, he saw a friend being chased by two older men. "He ran by yelling, 'Hey, Mouse! You gotta help me—these guys are going to kill me.' So when the two guys got close, I clotheslined the first one, hitting him so hard he smashed his cheek on the ground and was out cold, and I jumped on the second guy and had him on the ground ready to punch him in the face. In my stupor, I thought something wasn't right and a second later, the riot cops just jumped on me like crazy and pounded on me."

Up on Renfrew Street where Bradley Bennett was shaking off the blow to his head, he watched as the riot got more involved. "There were people starting to pull the rearview mirrors off cars parked along the street, and throw[ing] rocks and bottles. It was getting wild."

As the night set in, reinforcements from surrounding RCMP detachments in North Vancouver and Burnaby were dispatched. The sounds of screams, swearing, glass breaking, and police sirens echoed across the plaza. Rioters had filled empty wine bottles with gasoline at the station on the corner of Renfrew and Hastings and were now hurling Molotov cocktails at police vehicles. When one of the gasoline bombs hit a passing RCMP patrol car, it sent a sheet of flames high above the vehicle, while another exploded on the street. At one point, Bennett saw a young woman carrying a baby walk untouched through the no-man's land between police and the rioters and enter the Coliseum. Police feared the situation would worsen if the riot was not quelled by the end of the concert, when 17,000 fans would leave the Coliseum and potentially enter the fray. One officer told reporters on scene, "If we don't [clear the plaza], we are all dead."[43]

At eleven p.m., Constable Grant MacDonald was still standing firm on the riot squad line. "One thing I remember is how deafening the noise was with all the rioters yelling," he says. "At one point, rocks hit me in the helmet and the thigh at the same time, and I thought I'd been shot. It was nasty." The patience of the squad continued to be tested as police supervisors held them back, only temporarily moving the line forward to push rioters back to Renfrew Street.

Constable Bill Harkema was standing next to Grant MacDonald on the line. "I remember it all too well," he says of that night forty-four years later. "People were throwing rocks and bottles at us from Renfrew. I was standing next to big Grant, who is six-foot-four. People see him and maybe don't want to hit *him*, so they aim for the shorter guy next to him, and that was me," Harkema laughs. He had been on duty the night of the Gastown riot and was also on shift during the Sea Festival troubles. "We'd been taught crowd control, but each time we went out to deal with those riots, it wasn't a dedicated unit," he says. The Vancouver riot squad then was a pick-up squad of whoever happened to be on duty that night. There was no special riot squad uniform, so when a constable arrived on scene, he was directed to grab one of the general-issue white helmets (which didn't always fit) and a night stick. Squad members even wore their ties during riots—though at least the ties were clip-ons, which, in an altercation, would just break away.

Harkema concurs with MacDonald that the squad was held back for a pro-

43 Scott Honeyman and Bill Bachop, "Police Battle Mob at Stones Concert As Firebombs, Rocks, Bottles Hurled," *Vancouver Sun*, June 5, 1972, 1, 7.

longed period, as superiors "kept telling us to stand back and not do anything. We'd been held back as the rocks and bottles were being thrown at us, seeing some of our guys getting hurt, when they finally told us to charge—we'd had enough—and we charged like the charge of the goddamn Light Brigade." Grant MacDonald recalls the moment: "Finally, shortly after eleven p.m., our superintendent Ted Oliver gave the order and yelled, 'Get them!' and let us go." The riot squad ran into the crowd while VPD mounted police charged on horseback onto Renfrew Street.

Two East Enders arrested in the riot.
PHOTO: Dan Scott, *Vancouver Sun*

In addition to rocks, rioters had begun to throw flattened tin cans at the police, which bounced like skipping stones. Mac Ryan saw rioters overturn cars as police advanced on Renfrew Street. Columnist Allan Fotheringham, writing for the *Vancouver Sun*, noted, "As [police] approached, bottles, boulders, and sections of two-by-four torn from a fence pick them off. A constable staggers back, his face visor shattered by a rock."[44]

Ryan saw the constable get knocked down. Police charged and turned, rac-

44 Allan Fotheringham, "Untitled Column," *Vancouver Sun*, June 4, 1972.

ing in his direction. Ryan ran across Renfrew Street and up the front steps of a house, hoping the front door was unlocked—it was. As a mounted horseman charged onto the lawn with other police behind him, "I burst right through the door and ran through the fucking house. There's this poor family in their dining room, having their spaghetti dinner at the table, while the cops are right on my ass, and I run through the dining room and out the back door." Ryan kept running and fled into the alleyway. With his lungs on fire and almost out of breath, he ran nearly all the way back to Clark Park. "All I wanted to do was get out of there. But I'll never forget the look on that family's faces, sitting at the dining room table with napkins tucked in their shirts as I ran through," he says, laughing.

Within fifteen minutes, with the riot squad fully deployed, the Rolling Stones riot was all over—and just in time, as the concert was scheduled to end at 11:30 p.m. The band finished their set with (appropriately enough, considering what had been going on outside) "Street-Fighting Man." Thousands left the Coliseum and walked onto the plaza to head for home. Bewildered looks came over faces in the crowd as concert-goers picked their way over and around broken glass, torn shirts, ripped jackets, crushed eyeglasses, and overturned trash cans. As John Armstrong exited the arena, he wondered if the rapture had taken place outside while the concert was going on. "There was muttering in the crowd as we left that there had been a riot. I'd watched the Watts riots on TV, but I couldn't believe that a riot had happened here." Nick Jones was just as confused. "Nobody who was inside had any idea that something had taken place. Everybody was into the show, and nobody heard the police sirens outside."

The night wasn't over for Armstrong or his cousin Dennis. On the way to the bus stop, they stopped to ask someone on the sidewalk about what had happened. "My cousin Dennis took his pouch of Drum tobacco out of his jacket and started to roll a cigarette when a cop jumped out of nowhere and said, 'That's it, you're under arrest,' and he was in handcuffs." Armstrong and his cousin protested that it was only tobacco, but the officer wasn't interested, and took Dennis off to jail, threatening to take Armstrong along with him if he kept protesting the wrongful arrest. "I had to go to a pay phone and call my mom. You can imagine how that went. 'How was the show, dear?' 'Oh, good, Mom. Um, Dennis is in jail.' She asked what he was in for and when I told her it was for smoking a cigarette, she didn't believe it—'I hardly think he'd be in jail for just smoking a cigarette.' So my stepdad and mom had to drive in from White Rock. When we got down to the police station, Dennis was out on the sidewalk. When they impounded the evidence they realized what it was, kicked cousin Dennis out, and told him to get lost."

For both John Armstrong and Nick Jones in the crowd that night, the evening made for an early influential glimpse of the potential wild nocturnal pleasures of rock and roll. Before the decade was out, they would both go on to form their own legendary Vancouver bands, with Jones as the lead singer in the Pointed Sticks, and Armstrong the lead singer and guitarist in the Modernettes.

Most of the Clark Parkers had escaped arrest, including Bradley Bennett, who made it back to Clark Park around the same time Mac Ryan arrived. Others who had participated in the riot returned worse for wear after being clubbed by the riot squad. Paul Melo had actually made it into the Coliseum, but was unable to find any friends after the show and was just as confused as the other concertgoers who left the Coliseum that night, so he also drifted back to the Park.

"There was a moving and storage company on 12th Avenue," Bennett says. "We used to take the moving blankets out of the back of a truck and sleep under the trees in the Park and just bring them back in the morning so we could use them again." On what was left of a warm summer evening, the gang camped down for the night, trading war stories and eventually falling asleep under the stars in Clark Park.

However, the night was hardly over for Mouse Williamson, who had been arrested for fighting at the concert. He was dragged into the Showmart building, where police processed his arrest. "They had their command centre with desks in there, and all the riot squad gear," Williamson says. "They made me run a gauntlet of cops who hit or kicked me as I went down the row with handcuffs on me, and ran me into a desk where they made me sit for a while. Every time a cop asked what I was in for, the processing guy would yell, 'Assaulting a police constable,' and I'd get another backhand from the cop who'd asked. But I had no idea what they were talking about."

Williamson was transported to jail in a police wagon. The driver seemed to take the long route to the station, adding some sharp turns that earned Williamson a few more bruises as he was bounced around, handcuffed in the back of the wagon. "When I got to jail, I got kicked and punched a bit more. They put me in a thin cell nicknamed the Telephone Booth, where you couldn't lie down, and could only sort of stand up inside. By this time, the alcohol I'd drunk had really hit me, and I was taunting the police. I was hoping they'd just knock me out so I could get a night's rest. But I'd had enough of their shit already, and was yelling, 'I'll take you all on.' I punched the police from my cell as they tried to grab me. Finally they got me and pounded the piss out of me again. I don't remember much after that."

Williamson woke up the next morning hungover, sore, and unable to remember anything from the night before. Initially he'd thought he'd merely spent the night in the tank for being drunk in a public place. But as he tried to piece together the previous evening, a police officer escorted him out of his cell to handle some of his arrest paperwork. "I said to the guard, 'Hey, I guess I fucked up last night?' 'Yeah, you fucked up alright—you got arrested for assaulting a police officer.' It turns out that the guy I'd clotheslined on the plaza was a plainclothes police officer."

Looking down at a sheet of paper at the desk, he saw a mug shot of a man with his hair matted and filled with blood. "'Who's that poor fucker?' I asked, only to notice the name on the photo. It was me. I was so beat up, I didn't recognize myself."

The Rolling Stones riot made front-page headlines. And as the concert was the kickoff date for the Stones' North American tour, the riot made headline news across the continent. The *Vancouver Sun* quoted Police Inspector Frank Farley, a veteran of the Dieppe raid in World War II, who commented that he was disgusted at "Canadians fighting Canadians with Molotov cocktails."[45]

Media coverage was overwhelmingly favourable to the police. The level of chaos during the riot suggested it had been a wholly different kind of event than what had occurred in Gastown. The police department's strategy of inviting the media to stand among them during the riot ensured not only accurate but also sympathetic coverage, as reporters and police alike dodged rocks and bottles thrown at them. The reporters experienced first-hand what it was like to be in the middle of such a melee.

45 Allan Fotheringham, (untitled column), *Vancouver Sun*, June 5, 1972, 29.

Mouse Williamson and other rioters were not the only ones in rough shape the next day. The riot left thirty-one police injured, thirteen badly enough that they were taken on stretchers to hospital. Constable Stan Ziola suffered a cracked sternum after being hit with a railroad spike. Bill Harkema was also one of the injured, with a bruised ankle caused by a rock thrown at him as he stood on the riot squad line. "My foot swelled up pretty badly the next day," he says. "My ankle still smarts from it, but I'm seventy-three now, so it's just another ache. But that was a bad evening."

A total of twenty-two people were arrested on charges including possession of an explosive and a dangerous weapon—a four-foot-long logging chain with a hook on one end and a leather handle on the other. Another associate of the Clark Park gang, who'd been inside watching the show, was mistakenly arrested for throwing one of the Molotov cocktails outside and would spend six months in jail despite his innocence.

Gary Blackburn—who'd spent the previous day locked up with an unused Rolling Stones ticket in his pocket—watched that night as many of those arrested showed up at the jail. He was released the next day. He'd not only missed the concert, but now had a charge of drug possession on his record. Later, his friend confessed to the police that the jacket was his, and Blackburn's charge was dropped. "The whole thing was a waste of time, and I never got to see the Stones," he says.

In the days that followed, Vancouver police took the opportunity to both praise their own and point the finger at a new enemy. In an emotional statement at a press conference the following day, Police Superintendent Ted Oliver told reporters, "I'm proud of every one of those bastards I had working for me. They were cool, and they were very, very brave." Oliver alarmed some citizens and city council members by using language that some considered more befitting a soldier on the battlefield. But Oliver's emotion was forgivable, as most people admired the loyalty and respect in his statement. He further praised what he called "the professionalism of the riot squad," especially considering the "shaded image" they had received in the wake of the Gastown riot. "There is no way, ever, that I want to have to ask my men to go into a situation like that again," he said.

Speaking of the rioters, Oliver tersely noted: "This was a well-organized effort ... And they planned to cause real trouble if they got in [the Coliseum].

Had they got inside, there would have been a holocaust." Oliver stated that police believed there were up to five gangs involved in the riot, but Superintendent Tom Stokes would later specifically name the Clark Park gang as chiefly responsible.

When word reached the gang that police considered them the main culprits of the riot, Bradley Bennett says the news was greeted with astonishment and laughter. "The cops blew everything out of proportion. We were never that organized. They made it sound like we co-ordinated everything. It was ridiculous." Williamson agrees, and believes that it was likely the Youngbloods who had thrown the Molotov cocktails and smoke bombs. He insists to this day that none of the Clark Parkers attended the concert with an agenda to riot. "There were a bunch of Clark Parkers who even bought tickets and were inside when the whole thing happened. There was no agenda. It was all bullshit that we were behind the thing."

It seemed as if Vancouver police imagined that all the street gangs had come together that night and decided to attack the police. In truth, there had been no single faction responsible. Among the random East Enders, gate crashers, and drunken concertgoers with no gang affiliations, there were a number of gang members present, including members of the Riley Park gang, and a North Vancouver gang called the Lynn Valley Boys. But while the Clark Parkers were amused by the press attention and wore the badge of villainy with pride, some wondered why the police had been so prepared for the worst that night, with the riot squad at the ready. They were also curious why the police were so quick to accuse the Clark Parkers. Had they seen the photos in *The Grape* showing them with fists in the air, shouting "Power to the people"? Did the police presume they had joined forces with the Youngbloods and their Marxist revolutionary agenda? Or had complaints to police about the gang finally reached a tipping point so that they were now under greater scrutiny? How closely were they being watched?

Two days after the riot, a CBC television news interview was held on the Coliseum plaza—the scene of the battle, days earlier. Media liaison Jack Lee of the Pacific National Exhibition (PNE), which owned the Pacific Coliseum, stated, "There is a dissident element in this city who used the Rolling Stones concert as a venue for the trouble they wanted to make and succeed in making. I think had it not been for the bravery and restraint of the Vancouver city police and of the PNE staff, there would have been a lot more property damage and human suffering. We had meetings with police later to go over what had happened, and it was very definite that these were some of the gangs that they know about from throughout the city. So these aren't Rolling Stones fans—or what you call rock fans—these were a dissident element in the city who came to make trouble."[46]

When asked about the future of rock concerts in Vancouver, Lee said that the PNE board of directors had yet to decide. If Mayor Campbell imposed a ban, as he had publicly suggested, it would mean no large rock concerts would be booked in the city. And the PNE had the only venue large enough on which to stage them. Lee said that he knew Vancouver police were having their own meetings to discuss future strategy.

He concluded by stating: "Instead of just rock throwing, or throwing sticks of wood, now we have Molotov cocktails—which is a different matter entirely. The police were equipped, as you saw, with riot helmets and sticks. This is little enough to defend yourself from rocks, chunks of wood, and chains, but Molotov cocktails—now we're into a war situation."

Lee didn't know how true his words were about to become.

46 CBC Television News, Untitled film strip, dated June 5, 1972 (Vancouver, BC: CBC Vancouver Archives).

SEVEN: THE H-SQUAD

It was June of 1972, around the same time that a team of burglars was arrested in a botched robbery at the Watergate Hotel in Washington, DC, and a few days after the Rolling Stones concert. In Clark Park on a warm summer night, Gerry Gavin, Roger Daggitt, Albert Hill, and a kid named Phil Benson (name changed) were all drinking beer near the top of the pathway closest to Commercial Drive. The park was empty at that hour. It was a quiet weekday night, the silence broken only by the sound of the occasional vehicle driving along Commercial. The gang joked and drank and passed around a joint. Benson, more of a hanger-on than a real member of the gang, had brought a small battery-operated radio, and its tinny speaker played music from a local rock station.

Their conversation turned to various topics. Daggitt spoke of the Muhammad Ali fight six weeks earlier in Vancouver at the PNE where Ali had fought George Chuvalo. Gavin repeated a dirty joke that Mac Ryan had told him, and listed what he'd scored in a house burglary a few nights earlier. They listened to the music on Benson's radio, finished off the beers, and talked of maybe stopping off at Gary Blackburn's place on the way home. Gary's mother was kind and had always been okay with letting her son's friends crash at their family home rather than stay in the park all night. As Gary's sister Gail noted, "If we were going to drink and get up to no good, she'd rather have us do it at home, where she could keep an eye on us."

In a break in the conversation, Hill walked away from the others to urinate behind one of the nearby trees. As he zipped up his jeans, he turned around and saw a man in the dark standing several feet away, staring at him. "Jesus Christ—what are you doing?" Hill asked. "You watching me piss or something?!"

The man said nothing and continued to stare at Hill. The others, overhearing their friend's alarm, quickly walked over to see what was happening. The man stood partly in silhouette, lit unevenly by the street lamps off the Drive, which shone into the park through breaks in the tall trees. He was wearing cowboy boots and a corduroy jacket.

"What's your fucking problem, man?" Hill demanded.

The man moved slowly a few feet forward, stepping more into the light. He appeared older than them, perhaps in his late twenties or early thirties, and had a medium build. Benson turned off the radio he was holding, suddenly dropping the standoff into silence.

"We've met before," the man said casually. Hill looked around to see who he was looking at, but he seemed to be looking at all of them.

"Who the fuck are you? I don't know you, man," Hill said, now more angry than alarmed. "What the hell are you doing here? Get lost."

Benson thought he might be a Riley Parker, or because of the man's cowboy boots, one of the guys from the Out to Lunch Bunch he'd heard about. Maybe he was from some other street gang, looking for a fight. As Gavin and Daggitt stepped forward with fists clenched, three other men came out of the darkness behind them. In a brief scuffle, they violently grabbed Daggitt and Gavin, locking their arms behind their backs. Another man darted from the trees and grabbed Hill, twisting his arms back the same way. Benson saw that they were all about the same age as the first man, but noticeably bigger, and wearing jeans and boots. One had an old army jacket on and the other an old T-shirt. Roger Daggitt, then only eighteen, was already large and strong, and it took two of the men to hold his arms back. Benson began to panic and wondered how long the men had been there watching them.

Now, caught in the middle, he felt like he ought to run, but suddenly a firm hand on his shoulder jolted and froze him at the same time. It was the first man whom Hill had encountered in the darkness, but Benson was too scared to look him directly in the face. Instead, Benson looked off to see that Gavin, who had initially put up a struggle, had also given up more quickly than Daggitt had. That's when Benson noticed that Gavin had a revolver jabbed into the side of his ribs; the light from the street lamps reflected off the gun metal.

"I was going to tell you to get lost, kid," the man said to Benson. "But now I think you should stay and hear this." Addressing the group in a measured voice, he said: "You guys have to stay out of the park now. This is our park. You understand? It's over. Day or night. I don't fucking care. You're not hanging around here anymore. You got it?"

Daggitt, Gavin, and Hill said nothing, and Benson was too scared even to move. He then noticed that there was another man who must have been keeping an eye on the front entrance of the park in case someone unexpectedly walked up the path. He now came up to join them, but stayed back a distance and kept quiet.

A few silent moments passed. "Just so you understand ... Our gang is bigger than your gang. That's it," the man said, then turned to walk down the hill.

Hill was let go first, then was punched in the stomach by the man who had held him, and he fell forward. Then Daggitt was shoved away by the two men holding him. Gavin was let go last, but not before being backhanded in the head. Gavin swore and stepped forward as all of the men now walked away. One of them muttered, "Don't fucking be here again tomorrow night," then disappeared into the darkness of the park.

Benson, more confused and nervous than the others, watched as Hill stood up, getting his wind back. Gavin rubbed his head and swore. And while Benson didn't know Roger well, he looked angrier than Benson had ever seen him and made a motion to go after the men, but Gavin put out an arm to hold him back.

No one said anything for a few moments until Benson broke the silence, nervously at first and then more insistently. "What the fuck, man? Since when did the Riley Parkers pull shit like that or bring guns with them? Right into Clark Park? What the fuck, man? Let's go get them! They're probably still down on Commercial!"

"Shut up, Phil," Gerry Gavin said, cutting him off. "That wasn't the Riley Parkers. That was the cops."

Paul Stanton (name changed) woke up the day after the Rolling Stones riot to learn that many of his fellow police officers had been injured that night. Stanton himself had been off-duty that evening, and returned to his shift the following day. The riot was still very much the topic of conversation among other officers and around the police station.

Born in Ottawa in 1946, Stanton moved to Vancouver within a year of his birth. His family settled in South Vancouver at East 41st and Argyle. "I remember when that stretch of 41st Avenue was just two lanes with ditches on each side," he says. His father had served in the Royal Canadian Air Force and after the war, joined the VPD. Stanton attended Vancouver College, eventually following his father into the police department in 1968.

He had a strong and athletic build and had played rugby, lacrosse, and semipro football before he became a cop. With his burliness and a beard, Stanton earned the nickname "Grizz" later in his career because of his resemblance to actor Dan Haggerty from the TV series *The Life and Times of Grizzly Adams*. His first beat was in Gastown in 1969. "There were a couple of beer parlours there that always had problems," he says. "The New Fountain Hotel and the Stanley Hotel on Cordova Street had some of the roughest transvestites you'd ever seen. But overall, Gastown was pretty quiet then." By 1971, he was posted to East Vancouver. When he got called in to assist with drug enforcement in the area, he began to see some regular faces from around Clark Park.

In the early 1970s, heroin use was not uncommon, but cocaine was still too expensive to be seen regularly. More often, drug offences dealt with possession of LSD, methamphetamine, and most commonly, the open smoking of marijuana. Attitudes about marijuana have changed dramatically over the last several years, of course, and while its casual use is less of a priority for police today, in the early 1970s it was still a serious offence and a prosecutable crime. It was prevalent not merely at hippie Be-Ins and gatherings, but also on the streets, and certainly among the youth on Stanton's new beat in East Vancouver.

Stanton recalls seeing the symbol of the East Van cross. While the symbol originated in the 1940s, in East Vancouver in the 1970s it was particularly associated with east side gangs. "Nowadays, it seems almost accepted as the logo for East Vancouver," Stanton says. "But back then it was starting to show up all over the place. We were seeing it as graffiti on walls or among people we were dealing with [who] had it as a tattoo." Clark Park, too, became a regular focus on his beat.

"The Park is elevated [from the street], so you couldn't just drive by and see what was going on inside," Stanton says. Police usually parked on the surrounding streets and walked into the park, where they'd find the gang, often at the northeast side, near the main entrance. "In the beginning we pretty much left them alone. They weren't doing that much in the park itself, although they pretty much owned it," he says. "But the Rolling Stones concert was considered their coming out."

In the days after the Rolling Stones riot, Vancouver city council, citing security concerns, denied the permits for an upcoming Led Zeppelin concert at the Coliseum. The tour promoters were forced to book an additional date in Seattle that honoured the Vancouver tickets, and Led Zeppelin fans had to drive three hours south across the border to attend the show.

In addition, the city granted Vancouver police an additional budget of $21,000 for newer and more protective riot squad gear, and police began more focused training on crowd control. Mayor Tom Campbell personally lobbied for the riot squad to be equipped with longer riot sticks. They got new, thirty-six-inch (92-cm) police batons made from hickory wood to replace their old twenty-four-inch sticks. As far as the city was concerned, the Clark Park gang had nearly upended the Rolling Stones concert, forced the cancellation of Led Zeppelin's, and now required police to be armed and ready for them as never before. The riot served as a wakeup call.

As well, Paul Stanton was discreetly approached by supervisors to see if he'd be interested in moving to a special squad to deal with the park situation, and in particular the Clark Park gang. Sanctioned not only at the highest levels of the Vancouver Police Department, but according to former squad member Howard Corbett (name changed), also approved by BC Attorney General Leslie Peterson, the unit was given the responsibility to go after local youth gangs. They were apparently authorized to do so not only through criminal prosecution, but by whatever means it took to eradicate the gangs.

It is not known who conceived of the special squad. It wasn't likely the brainchild of then Police Chief John Fisk. "Fisk was a chief constable who had never walked a beat or rattled a doorknob," recalls legendary CKNW crime beat reporter George Garrett, who in a decades-long career, interviewed every Vancouver police chief who served in the latter half of the century. "He had been the top civilian employee and was promoted to chief when Ralph Booth retired." As an administrator, Fisk was not exceptionally well-liked by beat policemen; a stickler for etiquette, he insisted that constables wear their hats even while driving in their patrol cars.

A more likely origin might have been Police Superintendent Tom Stokes. Stokes had joined the police department at the age of twenty-three in 1939 and rose through the ranks to become deputy chief. "It was different on the beat then. If a cop got into trouble, people would come to his aid," Stokes recalled in a 1975 interview. "It's different now. I don't know why. The city's more dangerous for everyone. Drugs have a lot to do with it. And the whole mentality of the public seems changed. The courts are too lenient. They bend over backwards for a criminal."[47]

George Garrett recalls that Stokes was well regarded within the department. "Tom had an expression he often used," he says. "He called many guys 'pally,' as in pal. I knew him when he was a staff sergeant in the investigation division, sometimes working four-to-midnight shifts. I recall a spate of hold-ups that took place in the 1950s. I heard Stokes say to his guys, 'That sounds like so-and-so,' and name a suspect. He told his guys to pick him up. I can't recall if they got the right man, but it showed me that he knew how some criminals likely operated."

If there was opposition to the squad being formed, it is unrecorded. Some may have disagreed with the broad powers given to the squad, but there was a general feeling amongst not only the department but the public as well that it was no longer enough for police to simply pick up the offenders and have them taken to juvenile detention. The youthful gang members were becoming adults as well as graduating to more serious crimes. Even if the Clark Parkers had not diabolically plotted the 1972 Rolling Stones riot, hadn't been the main instigators behind the chaos of the Rock and Roll Revival concert in 1971, even never been the culprits behind the nightly violence that interrupted the Sea Festival in 1970, something had to be done about the burglaries, fights, vandalism, arsons, and general disruption caused throughout the East End. "There were a lot of people living in fear in the [Clark Park] neighbourhood," said Howard Corbett. "People were being brutalized there, either verbally or physically. Their homes were being broken into, there were assaults and arsons going on." Because so many police had been injured during the Rolling Stones riot, they decided to focus on the activities of the Clark Park gang, and they could no longer employ half-measures.

Formally coined as the Task Force on Youth and Park Problems, beat police referred to the special squad as the "Heavy-Squad," or "H-Squad" for short. It was made up of a mix of young and older officers, pulled mostly from the Hastings Street and Granville Street beats. Many already had some plain-clothes policing experience or worked undercover in the drug squad, but all knew this would be a unique detail. The existence of the eleven-man team was not formally made known to the public, though the group was no secret in police quarters or according to police memoranda.

47 Mike McCardell, "Stokes Recalls Days of Street Justice," *The Province*, October 7, 1975.

For his part, Paul Stanton joined the new squad without reservation. "I was young at the time, and open to pretty well anything," he says. "You have to understand that policing in the 1970s was a lot different from now. Almost all our supervisors and sergeants had military experience—they'd served in the war—[and therefore] there was a different attitude and tone about policing, a sort of 'just get the job done' attitude. Everything regarding oversight was looser. There weren't really internal investigations back then. It was a wilder time."

Police Superintendent Tom Stokes (pictured here in this undated photo) was aware of the H-Squad and may have assisted in selecting members of the team.
PHOTO: Deni Eagland, *Vancouver Sun*

The 1982 Canadian Charter of Rights and Freedoms significantly strengthened the rights of criminal defendants and tightened rules around how police procured evidence. In general, police rules and oversight were more rigorous. But in those wilder, pre-Charter years, sometimes police took shortcuts on blatantly guilty suspects. However, the mandate of the new unit raised eyebrows even then.

"The fear was it was only going to get worse," says Corbett. "So our job was to go after the gangs, and one way or the other have them stay out of the parks and no longer allow them to be the problems they'd become. Jail wasn't a strong enough deterrent, and if that meant doing something else, so be it."

"They were tough and strong," says seventy-four-year-old retired constable Vern Campbell. "Christ, if you were under six-foot-three, you were only able to serve coffee to these guys." He'd spent most of his policing career on robbery and homicide squads, but knew the H-Squad members personally and professionally over the years before he retired in 1994.

Paul Stanton was one of the bigger men on the squad, but not as big as "Big John" Flaten. At age forty-one, he was one of the older men in the H-Squad, but standing six-foot-three and weighting about 280 pounds (127 kg), his size more than made up for his age. A long-time weightlifter who could have given Doug Hepburn a run for his money, Flaten held the dead-weight lift record in Vancouver for years. With his Norwegian ancestry, at another time in history he might have been a Viking. Flaten joined the Vancouver Police Department in 1953, and was a personable and well-liked police officer whose career lasted thirty years. As one retired constable who worked alongside Flaten recalled, "Everybody agreed that he was the kind of guy you'd like to have around when the shit hit the fan."

Not all of the squad were as big as Flaten or Stanton, but almost all were strong and had athletic backgrounds. Three had been present at the Rolling Stones riot and sustained scrapes, cuts, and bruises.

The leader of the new unit was Joe Cliffe. Cliffe had spent most of his early career in robbery and homicide investigations and his later years in the major crimes division. He is remembered as a well-respected member of the police department, a good investigator, and a man who could get results. "Joe was a serious guy when he needed to be, but had a good sense of humour," said one police officer (who does not wish to be named) who worked with him. A handsome outdoorsman and avid fisherman, Cliffe was equally at home policing the streets of Vancouver as he was fishing on the Chilcotin River at his cabin in the British Columbia interior.

"He was our boss, and the corporal. Everything went through Joe," Stanton notes, recalling that Cliffe also perhaps shielded the squad from internal politics. "If there was any negative feedback or complaints about what we were doing, we didn't hear it. Maybe Joe never even saw it; it was quickly handled up the ladder." Cliffe and the squad were protected and isolated so they could get the job done, and as quickly as possible.

The VPD's H-Squad remains one of the more guarded secrets in the history of the Vancouver Police Department. Little information was recorded or filed about its mandate. The poor filing techniques and an absence of digital records makes material from the early 1970s difficult to find in the VPD archive; only major crimes such as unsolved homicides are retained from that era. In 2016, the author filed a Freedom of Information request to the VPD, but no surviving records or reports from the H-Squad appear to remain. This is the first time members of the squad have spoken publicly about the posting.

Curiously, the only record from the Heavy Squad can be found in the public archives of the Vancouver Police Museum. It is a photo of the eleven-member plainclothes squad in a mock police line-up. Many of the officers are smiling or laughing for the camera, giving the impression that the photo was taken for their own amusement, not for official records. How this photo of the squad ended up in the Museum's collection is unknown.

The VPD H- Squad, 1970s. Among them: #16 John Flaten, #17 Joe Cliffe, and #20 Jim Maitland.
PHOTO: Vancouver Police Museum, PO2892

Perhaps one reason why the squad seems amused is because they were being photographed as undercover plainclothes officers—though donning some of the clothing of the period means their clothes were hardly plain. "Polyester shirts were big back then of course," Stanton says with a laugh. "Some of the officers wore flared jeans and sort of hippie-style clothing. It was very early 1970s counterculture." He says that he would rarely have gone out in public dressed that way if off-duty. "The idea was, we'd dress to fit in with the park, and if anybody saw in us there and a fight broke out, we'd just look like another gang. The main thing was that we fit in—and it was no different from undercover drug work that way."

In keeping with the '70s fashions, Stanton also recalls that everyone in the squad grew beards, goatees, or Fu Manchu style moustaches. While Joe Cliffe's daughter, Holly, never spoke with her father directly about the H-Squad, she says: "My memories are of how they all had to grow beards and 'look scary.' There was lots of kidding around about how these normally clean-cut policemen had to look like thugs!"

Stanton recalls carrying a small flashlight with him on some nights in the park, but adds, "The two things you never went without were your firearm or your handcuffs." Squad members often had their guns in a shoulder holster or underneath their shirt.

The H-Squad worked the evening shifts almost exclusively, but rarely was the entire eleven-man team on duty all at once. Instead, four to six officers at a time would do a shift, breaking up into two-man teams that drove in unmarked cars past houses where the Clark Parkers lived. "There were a lot of hangers-on, so we went looking for the core gang members," Stanton says. "If we found them on the street or if they were in a car driving around, we'd radio it in to our guys and set up a surveillance to see what they were up to. If they gathered in Clark Park, we'd show up, park our cars, and take a walk in there." Police sirens and lights (hidden from sight in ghost cars) were never used unless it was to pull over a car. Nor did the squad ever run into the park yelling "Police!" They didn't need to—everyone knew that the H-Squad were cops.

The Clark Parkers do not remember them fondly. "They'd show up and just say, 'Okay, who are we taking in tonight?'" recalls Gary Blackburn. "But a lot of us back then could slip out of a pair of handcuffs. You'd flex your wrists as they put them on, and then relax them once you had them on. But then they started putting handcuffs on so tight that they'd cut into your skin, or else use two pairs at once."

Blackburn and the others were used to cops arresting or questioning them in the park, but noticed that the attitude of police changed after the Rolling Stones riot. One evening, the squad raced into the park in their ghost cars, slamming on their brakes in front of the gang. "They were like bikers," says Mac Ryan. "They almost ran us over! We knew they were cops, but not at first, when they showed up like that. I had some weed on me, and I didn't feel like going to jail, so I ran around to the back of the field house. The weed was in a cigarette pack, and I threw it on the roof. When I walked back, one [squad member] grabbed me and hit me in the gut." Tossed into one of the ghost cars, Ryan was driven down to the waterfront. "They threatened me that they could do this and that or just kill me and dump my body somewhere and it would never be found."

The H-Squad initially used scare tactics, tough language, and all manner of verbal intimidation to get their message across, but sometimes the interactions turned more vulgar—and more physical. "There were three of them in the car—one driving and the two who had me sandwiched in the back seat," says Ryan. "One next to me let go a big fart, and he started to laugh, saying, 'Oh man, smell that one. I had too much beer last night!' They're all laughing and then they start to hit me over the head with little blackjack clubs they had. I thought, *Fuck, these guys are crazy.*"

Sometimes more devious techniques were used. Bradley Bennett remembers when members of the H-Squad would walk past a group of Clark Parkers and single out one person to thank them for information they'd supposedly provided to the cops. This was done loudly, so the rest overheard; it was part of a strategy to foment discord and questions of loyalty amongst the gang members.

Many surviving Clark Parkers who recall this period insist that they were given overly hostile treatment, especially when the squad's initial scare tactics didn't persuade them to quit hanging around the park. "They would pick you up, drive you out to Steveston or someplace hard to get back from, kick you out of the car and leave you there. If that didn't work, you'd just get an old-fashioned beating," Bennett says. Clark Parker John Twynstra encountered the H-Squad one night and received a beating that kept him recuperating at home for a week.

From this sudden change in tone of policing around the park, rumours began to spread that off-duty police officers had formed a vigilante squad to go after the Clark Parkers. It was difficult for some to fathom that such a squad was officially sanctioned. Allegations of police abuse raised by Clark Park gang members are not to be wholly disbelieved. Paul Stanton candidly admits, "I don't remember [picking up suspects and kicking them out of squad cars far from the park] personally. But I do know it was done in general back then.

That sort of thing wouldn't have been uncommon for the time. If you had a problem and you couldn't do anything about it, you'd pick them up and drop them off in one end of town and let them walk back. That certainly isn't done anymore. But, obviously, the whole squad itself isn't the kind of thing that would or could be done anymore."

Occasionally, the tactics backfired. Clark Parker Mark Owens recalls being picked up one night at the park by the squad. "Some B & E had just happened in the area, so they went to grab whoever they could grab," he says dismissively. "They took me down to the Fraser River, threw me in, and took off. I was so far away from the park, I had to steal a car just to get back home!"

How aggressive the H-Squad, or police in general, became with the Clark Park gang is difficult to ascertain. The police didn't admit to several of the accusations made by the Clark Park gang, and some individual allegations may be exaggerated. Many living members of the H-Squad, who have long since retired, declined to be interviewed for this book. Some now have children or family members in the Vancouver Police Department and don't wish to make them feel uncomfortable. Others declined to speak about the H-Squad, arguing that they were using typical policing methods of the period. Most feel that they now have little to gain by publicly answering criticisms for their actions in the Wild West days of policing.

Rumours and allegations persist that police in the squad used rough treatment and intimidation to control gang members. Stories abound about gang members being thrown off the docks into Burrard Inlet, and live rounds shot into the water. Once they'd been pulled out, they were told never to enter the park again. Another unconfirmed rumour has it that one evening, the H-Squad marched into the park with baseball bats to fight with the gang members.

The most extreme stories and incidents are difficult to corroborate. Paul Stanton disavows rumours about battles or serious physical altercations with the gang. And he insists that as soon as the H-Squad began its raids into the park, "They were intimidated right from the beginning, and stopped hanging out [there]. They got low-key pretty quickly. In fact, soon they were spread out all over the place and we had trouble finding them."

Certainly, any physical abuse alleged by the gang members could have occurred at the hands of squad members other than Stanton or on shifts for which he was not on duty. He does not recall the kinds of altercations that some Clark Parkers say occurred. Other police officers, including regular patrols, the undercover drug squad, and even the RCMP, were all active in the area at the time and may have played a hand. The gang members themselves make little distinction between those known to be beat police and H-Squad members, and tend to lump together all police they encountered at the time.

H-Squad member Howard Corbett does recall a significant fight at the Drake Hotel on Powell Street. One night an altercation that began in the bar spilled out to the parking lot, and a crew of pool cue-swinging Clark Parkers were subdued with an "aggressive response" by the H-Squad—a response that Corbett declined to elaborate on.

Bradley Bennett with Roger Daggitt and friends at the Biltmore Hotel pub, 1973.
PHOTO: Courtesy of Bradley Bennett

"They always came in bunches," former gang member Gary Blackburn says. "They didn't have the balls to come two at a time. They had better sense. One time, we fought back. That freaked them out. So they never came in looking for us with just two people."

By July 1972, the heat from police was so great that the gang refrained from hanging out at the park. Members either gathered at individual homes or, now that many were of legal age, at bars like the Biltmore Hotel, the Eldorado, Lasseter's Den, the Blue Boy Hotel pub, or the Vanport Hotel. As a result, the

H-Squad began to harangue individual Clark Parkers on the street.

"They always wanted to know who 'the leader' was," Blackburn says. "That was always the biggest fucking joke—there was no leader. We never had one. The scene was, if you wanted to do something, you just went ahead and did it. There weren't any rules or some code to go do this or that. We were 'organized' to the extent that we stuck up for each other, and if you tried to fuck with one of us, you were going to fuck with everybody."

"The H-squad knew where everybody lived. You couldn't go anywhere after a while," remembers Mac Ryan who, even at the worst of times, dealt with the squad irreverently. "They'd come into the nightclubs that we'd started to go to and stop and question me. I'd say, 'I'm the leader on Tuesday. No, wait a minute, I'm on Thursday, somebody else is tonight, and another guy is tomorrow.' I'd tell them the leader's name was 'Jack,' and when then the cops would ask what his last name is, I'd say 'Me-off.'" Ryan's impudence inevitably earned him another rough midnight ride in the back of an H-Squad car.

However aggressive the squad's tactics might have been, their success was also quickly noted by many who lived around the park who had seen their neighbourhood decline. Retired constable Vern Campbell remembers, "An old lady who lived across from Clark Park was talking to a uniformed officer one day and he asked her how things were going in the park. She said things were much better since the 'older' gang arrived!"

While the Clark Parkers might have temporarily abandoned the park, the H-Squad also seemed to embitter the hangers-on and others who were on the gang's side or who were merely anti-police. It was believed that the police had gone above the law to get rid of the gang. "They couldn't beat us fairly. So they had to invent a goon squad to try to put pressure on us. That didn't stop us. It just made everybody more pissed off," says Mouse Williamson, who thought the tactics of the squad upset what he and others in the East End regarded as the code of the streets. "It's like cops and robbers; if you get caught fair and square—that's the way it goes. We're supposed to be the liars, cheaters, and schemers, not those guys. They're supposed to be honest, and do things by the book, but they threw the fucking book away on us."

Some might have thought that the Clark Parkers were now getting a taste of their own medicine. If there was any doubt that the gang was under more police scrutiny, there was no question after June 27, when, at 8:30 in the morning, police began a roundup of drug traffickers across the city. By lunchtime, twenty offenders were in jail. Eighty-two warrants were issued in one day for charges of trafficking heroin, marijuana, hashish, and LSD; the crackdown was the conclusion of a five-month undercover police investigation. More arrests were made in the following days.

The arrests were front-page news in the evening edition of the *Vancouver Sun*; the article stated that while those arrested included some residents of Gastown, the overwhelming majority was from East Vancouver. Their names, occupations, and the charges against them were listed. Cooks, longshoremen, housewives, and landscapers were among those accused, as well as two who were well-known to Clark Park: a thirty-year-old Vancouver fireman by the name of David Ashlee and twenty-nine-year old Robert McIvor, the caretaker of Clark Park, both arrested for trafficking hashish.

McIvor and his girlfriend were a well-liked hippie couple who lived in the caretaker's house in Clark Park (which later burned down). It was no secret around the park that they could buy hashish from the couple. The Clark Parkers also knew that Ashlee was a hash and marijuana dealer as well as a city fireman.

The officer primarily involved with the investigation might have stayed undercover longer than the five-month period he'd managed, but police began to be concerned that he would soon be found out. When his identity was revealed, those in the Clark Park scene were surprised to discover that the officer was a twenty-five-year-old police constable named Ken Doern. Those around the park had known him by a different name. In the months before the Rolling Stones riot, he was seen around the park trying to buy marijuana. Then, he was known as Ken Bell.

Doern was born in Winnipeg in 1946. He joined the Vancouver Police Department in 1971, and early the following year, when his face was still not yet known on the streets, he was appointed to the undercover vice-squad to infiltrate the Clark Park gang. "Ken was a good guy, but he'd rush into things," said one officer who worked with him. "He once interrupted a stake-out that he stumbled into and rushed to make arrests, not realizing what had been going on."

Dale Matthew, then a teenaged girl who hung around the park with the gang, recalls Doern being around that spring. "He was a really nice guy. I always wondered why at the end of the night at parties, he would drive me and my friend Sue home; he'd always just happen to be in the area," she says. Dale was unaware that Doern was an undercover policeman. "He was always asking 'Why are you hanging around those guys?' We told him that they were like our brothers or our family. I think after a while he knew that he wouldn't get any answers from us about what the guys were up to, but he still wanted to make sure we got home okay."

Doern's cover story, apparently, was that his job was to drive around the streets and report problems with the roads, such as potholes. This allowed him the mobility of a car and the ability to surveil around Clark Park and East Vancouver at large, making friends and contacts, and later reporting back on activities involving the drug deals in and near the park.

Before the Rolling Stones concert, Doern learned that the Clark Park gang had met with the Youngbloods at their home, and though he wasn't present at that meeting, he reported to his superiors that the gangs had connected and were all going to attend the concert. Either suspecting that the gang had a master plan, or having just overheard that some individual gang members were going to try to crash the gates, Doern apparently reported that an incident should be expected. Acting on this intelligence, Vancouver police officials decided in advance that the riot squad would be ready and waiting for whatever happened that night at the Coliseum.

"I remember meeting Ken," says Mouse Williamson. It wasn't long after the Stones concert when Doern visited the Williamsons' home. "I was down in my basement sleeping when some people brought over this guy who said his name was Ken Bell. They vouched for him and said he was cool. Doern wanted to buy weed. I didn't sell it. I didn't even have any to give him, but one of my friends there named Jimmy Smith told Ken he could buy from [David] Ashlee, who lived up the street." Police records suggest that Williamson's family home had come under the radar of Doern and the H-Squad.

In a confidential VPD surveillance report addressed to Staff Sergeant Devries of the drug squad, Doern states that ten members of the gang met in the Williamson home to discuss the amount of recent police activity in the area. Doern notes that "Dave ASHLEE and Robert McIVOR are reportedly selling large amounts of hashish to members of the gang." The report also states that Williamson was in possession of a gun owned by one Doug Flood, a doorman at the El Dorado Hotel beer parlour: a .45 semi-automatic with two clips of bullets.[48]

— CONFIDENTIAL —

VANCOUVER POLICE DEPARTMENT

DETECTIVE

DIVISION

TO S/Sgt. Devries DRUG SQUAD DATE June 13/72.

RE: CLARK PARK GANG

Received info that B.J. BROSGART and teh (10) other u/k male youths met with Danny WILLIAMSON, SNELGROVE and the SMITHs in WILLIAMSONS basement today at 12;30 p.m. This group of youths made a number of phone calls (n.k. to whom) re the recent police activity in the area. C.P.L.T. has a camera and flash provided by ASHLEE.

Joanne LaFORGE, the sister of Leonard Earnest LaFORGE @ "FIDDLER" has been hanging around the SMITH and WILLIAMSON residences with some members of the NANAIMO-PROJECT GANG, n.k. to the u/s.

Danny WILLIAMSON had FLOOD's .45 semi-auto pistol, o.l. approx. 8-10", with two (2) clips and about 25-30 rounds. The u/s was unable to see the Serial No. of the weapon.

Dave ASHLEE and Robert McIVOR are reportedly selling large amounts of Hashish to members of the C.P.L.T.

Dennis Turner @ YANDLE is planning on getting rid of his Marihuana plants, because of the recent police activity. These plants maybe transported via Jimmy SMITH's truck or Dennis (david) SCHAFFER's Blk/Red Charger Conv. B.C.L. JGK-300. SCHAFFER now lives in New Westminster - address n.k.

No definite plans have been made for any demonstration, June 18 re the cancellation of the Led ZEPPLIN Concert. At this time I don't think members of the C.P.L.T. or Nanaimo Project Gang will be participating in any great numbers at the Coliseum June 18/72

This confidential 1972 VPD memo details ongoing surveillance of Mouse Williamson and other members of the Clark Park gang.
SOURCE: Courtesy of the author

"When I got picked up by the goon squad, they'd push me around and say, 'So, you think you're tough and you're going to shoot a cop?' But I didn't know what they hell they were talking about," Williamson says. Williamson saw the information in the report for the first time during interviews for this book, and was shocked to discover both its existence and its details. "Suddenly, it all makes sense to me what the goon squad had been telling me all those years ago.

48 "Vancouver Police Memorandum: Confidential: June 13th, 1972. To Sgt. Devries, Drug Squad. Re: Clark Park Gang."

They thought I had a gun and was ready to use it." It wasn't his, and he insists he'd swear under oath today that he had never had a gun in his possession at the time.

But it didn't matter. As far as the police were concerned, he had a gun and they felt he was ready to shoot the police. Danny "Mouse" Williamson was a marked man. And now, they wouldn't wait around for the Clark Park gang to show up at the park or at another concert. They would take the battle to the park themselves.

EIGHT: THE SUMMER OF '72

On Friday, June 23, 1972, a party was in full swing in a ground-floor apartment near Fraser Street and East 59th Avenue in South Vancouver. Among the thirty to forty men and women who filled the apartment were some well-known Clark Parkers, including Gary Blackburn, Mac Ryan, Mouse Williamson, Gerry Gavin, Wayne Angelucci, Rob Thacker, Coke Singh, and Albert Hill, as well as few guys from the Renfrew Park scene who'd come along with them. The party had reached that late-night stage when enough strangers had shown up that no one in attendance seemed to be quite sure whose party it was or if the host was still there.

Something different seemed to be happening in each corner of the room: One couple made out by the avocado-green curtains that covered a screen door; two men sat on a harvest-gold couch, rolling joints and debating about what was happening in Vietnam, including the famous *New York Times* photo that had come out just a week earlier of a young girl running naked on a road after being severely burned by napalm; another man lay passed out in a chair near the hi-fi stereo. On the white kitchen counter, amidst a forest of empty stubby beer bottles, was an ashtray filled to the brim. And all around, people talked and laughed, drank, smoked weed, and danced to the music.

At one point, Gerry Gavin took over the hi-fi and put on R. Dean Taylor's 1970 criminal-on-the-lam AM radio hit "Indiana Wants Me," then a favourite on the jukebox at Ben's Café. Gavin yelled, "This one's for Bennett!" which brought laughter and toasts among the East Enders in the room, as Bradley Bennett was in jail. Gavin then orchestrated the party-goers to wildly chime in with the chorus.

But the drunken smiles soon broke into looks of confusion when there was a loud pounding on the front door. Constables Bob Munro and George Izatt had been dispatched to the address in response to a noise complaint in the building. "They came to the door and told us to break the party up," recalls Mouse Williamson. "Of course, we didn't think we were making all that much noise, and we didn't want to end it."

The din was hushed for a few minutes after the police had delivered their warning. But by the time the constables returned to their car, the noise from the apartment had returned to its original level. Munro and Izatt looked at each other and turned to go back into the building when two bottles exploded by their vehicle—someone at the party had hurled a couple of stubbies out of the window at the police car. With so many people inside, there wasn't much sense in the two of them heading back to the apartment on their own, so Munro and Izatt radioed dispatch and called for backup. Dispatch sent a team of officers, including constable Esko Kajander, who had joined the police department four years earlier at the age of twenty-two.

A Vancouver police constable on Granville Street, 1970.
PHOTO: Vancouver Police Museum, P02027

Born in Tampere, Finland, Esko Kajander moved with his family to Canada in 1959. He became a police officer because "it was something I'd always wanted to do," Kajander says, his English still inflected by a slight Finnish accent.

Kajander was given the usual treatment that a wet-behind-the-ears police officer can expect in the first year of duty. "You were called a 'piss kid'—but usually only by officers a couple of years older than you. The older ones were more relaxed; some of them were veterans of the war, tail gunners or pilots. As long as you realized that you didn't know anything and you just listened and got along, you were made to feel like one of the crew. Anyone fresh out of the academy who started to order other officers around didn't go far."

Kajander entered the world of policing at a time when technology played far less of a role in the job than it does today; 1970s police equipment was comparatively rudimentary. While constables had radios in their patrol cars, on their beats they needed to carry large walkie-talkie-style radios. Kajander's first beat was on Granville Street downtown. If he encountered suspects or noticed suspicious activity, he would take down names by hand in a notebook. "Later, you'd go for a coffee break and use the café phone to call for a criminal record check on the names," Kajander explains. "There was a VPD criminal records office, but it was closed at night, so most of the time you had to call the RCMP Crime Index at the old post office building at 15th and Main. They had giant rolodexes there; they could look up a record for you and give you extra information over the phone, or compare dates of birth to make sure you had the right person. If you wanted a photo, they could mail a black-and-white photo to you, which you'd pick up at the police station the next day. That's how we had to do it back then."

In the late 1960s and early '70s, new constables were provided with a belt for the police-issued .38 handgun worn on the left, a belt pocket for handcuffs, and a bullet loop that held six extra rounds of ammunition. That, along with two pairs of uniform pants, a shirt, and a tunic, were required dress from September to May. They were each given a heavy wool peacoat for bad weather, and whenever officers were outside, they had to wear their hats.

For a time, Kajander worked under the command of Sam Andrews, a VPD legend from the homicide department, known as an-old school master investigator. Andrews assigned Kajander to do the specialized kind of undercover work called "cell sitting," which required considerable patience and confidence. Sitting in a jail cell with an offender, acting as if he had been arrested himself, Kajander would draw out details of the crime in conversation, which could result in a confession.

"The best was if you were in a cell overnight. I would at first just ignore them. As soon as I was in the cell, I'd climb onto my bunk and go to sleep. It would drive people nuts if you didn't want to talk, especially if they'd been in there for hours by themselves already. Sometimes, if they started talking, I'd even tell them to shut up at first. They'd always ask what you were in for, and you'd always tell them it was a violent crime or something they could relate to or considered serious. Eventually, you'd ask them what they were doing there, and then the whole story, with all the details, would pour out. It always worked."

By 1972, Kajander was stationed at "the District," a police substation at 45th Avenue and Ash Street in South Vancouver that had opened in 1961 to meet the expanding demands of policing beyond the downtown core. Kajander was at the District when the call came on the radio that Munro and Izatt needed additional officers to attend to the party on Fraser Street.

Called "the District" by VPD officers, the Oakridge Police Substation stood at 45th Avenue and Ash.
PHOTO: Vancouver Police Museum, PO7970

"When we arrived, there were already a half dozen police there," Kajander recalls. "The party-goers were still throwing bottles from the windows of the apartment. There was a lot of chatter on the radio while this was going on, so police all over the area heard about it, and others started to show up, including the guys from the H-Squad." As additional police readied themselves on Fraser Street, Joe Cliffe, John Flaten, and two other members of the H-Squad joined them. Police held back for several minutes, according to Kajander, waiting for a supervisor to arrive and give orders.

The party crowd began to taunt police from the apartment windows and behind the screen door. Mac Ryan yelled at police, "You'll never take us sober!" causing a burst of laughter from inside the apartment, and perhaps even eliciting reluctant smiles from the police. While a few people inside sensed trouble and headed for the back exit, most remained—not sober enough or perhaps too stoned to realize that they were teasing a cobra. More bottles were thrown from the apartment, hitting the street and sidewalk, as the noise inside continued unabated. Someone put "Down on the Street" from The Stooges' *Fun House* album on the stereo and turned up the volume while a stoned couple danced in the living room, oblivious to what was happening outside.

Taunts and bottles continued to fly as police car headlights aimed at the front of the apartment building illuminated the faces of those at the windows. Neighbours began to peek out from behind curtains to see what was happening. On the party's stereo, Iggy Pop's voice whooped and hollered, underscoring the tense and unpredictable summer evening.

For a moment if felt like a standoff until it was suddenly interrupted. Both Wayne Angelucci and Mouse Williamson believe that police finally charged when one officer was struck with a bottle. Kajander remembers that a supervisor ordered police to start making arrests. Regardless, all of a sudden police began to flood into the building. "I don't know what caused it," says Gary Blackburn. "But the next thing you know, police were all over the place and all hell broke loose."

"We kicked the door in. It was total chaos and packed in there," remembers Kajander. "They were all fighting back. Nobody went quietly, and furniture was flying everywhere. We fought for half an hour." At one point, Kajander was barricaded in the bathroom while fighting two men, the door blocked by others fighting and pushing outside it. He wrestled his opponents in the narrow space until he finally managed to shove the door open enough for fellow constable Stan Joplin—who was handcuffing someone—to toss him a rubber truncheon. With weapon in hand, Kajander was able to subdue, handcuff, and arrest the two men.

When the chaos hit the living room, the record player was finally kicked over, cutting the music as police attempted to grab and handcuff as many as they could. As Mouse Williamson was fleeing the living room, a police officer rammed him head-first through the screen door. "It almost knocked me out. I was still stunned from the knock on the head, but I ran outside, and everybody was running in every direction." After getting away from the building, Williamson realized that he'd left his jacket behind. Fearing that his jacket with his ID would be found and he could be picked up, he ran back around the corner to Fraser Street.

Meanwhile, uniformed police and H-Squad officers outside were fighting to arrest Clark Parkers on the front lawn. "I'll never forget it," says Wayne Angelucci. "One of the police dogs had me, and I don't know if I kicked at it or pushed it away, but that's when a cop kicked me in the chest. I went down. I could hardly breathe."

Williamson somehow evaded detection and entered the apartment, grabbed his jacket, and rushed out the back door. With regrettable timing, he turned the corner just as another man was running in the opposite direction. "I saw a cop had been chasing after a guy, but he'd run out air. The guy took off, and the cop stood with his hands on his knees, trying to catch his breath, when he looked up and saw me right in front of him. I said, 'I guess you're taking me in?' and with that he threw the handcuffs on me, and that was that."

Police wagons driven by constables Pat Laughy and Ron Palm arrived, and those arrested were taken to the District. Handcuffed with his hands in front of him, Williamson was taken into one of the wagons where another of the arrested party-goers produced a bag of MDA. The men passed the bag around in an effort to dispose of the drugs before they arrived at the station. "We were already high and drunk, but by the time we got to [the station in] Oakridge we were high as kites."

The District had only five jail cells, each connected to the other, and was not equipped to hold large numbers of prisoners at one time. As those taken away from the Fraser Street party showed up to be booked, they were placed in cells with four to five people already in them. From there, police escorted each person to a booking room and photographed them with an arresting officer for evidence to be used at a later court hearing.

"If, as an officer, you were in a picture, you had something to do with the arrest," Kajander says. But to Mouse Williamson, the booking process seemed much less coherent. "It felt almost like an auction." Williamson recalls that police loudly called out the name of each prisoner as he was about to be booked. "They were all saying 'Who wants this guy,' 'I'll take him,' or 'No, I want him!'"

The photos of the booking, discovered in the archives of the Vancouver

Constable Jim Yohimas looks on as constables Gary Hayworth (left) and Gary Campbell (right) stand near Wayne Angelucci for an arrest processing photo.
PHOTO: Vancouver Police Museum, N00582A

Constable Pat Laughy stands with Danny "Mouse" Williamson.
PHOTO: Vancouver Police Museum, N00582N

Police Museum during the research for this book, are published here for the first time. Some show Clark Parkers Angelucci, Williamson, and Thacker photographed next to their arresting officers as well as H-Squad's Joe Cliffe and also John Flaten, who is shown with a young offender who appears to have urinated himself—perhaps not an uncommon reaction from offenders arrested by the big man.

"Back in our cells, we started raising hell," Williamson says. "They got so pissed off they shut the lights off. We went apeshit, so they turned them back on again. That's when they brought Gerry in."

Gerry Gavin and Wayne Angelucci's ride to the District had taken a strange turn. "Gerry had all this LSD and mescaline on him. He didn't want to get busted for it, so he just took it all," Angelucci says. "By the time they got him to jail, he went nuts. He was so high, they couldn't stop him." As Gavin was escorted out of the police wagon, he fought back, and it took four officers to hold him. He struggled with his handcuffs, trying to hit the officers, who started to punch him. Gavin, now completely smashed, yelled, "I love you guys. I'm the Lord Jesus Christ! You can't hurt me! Jesus loves you!" The jail cells erupted in derisive laughter as those already booked watched police try to contain Gavin, who tried to light a bunkbed on fire as soon as he was put in a cell.

"Gerry was always like that. If he got whacked by a cop, he wouldn't take their shit. He'd try to punch cops in the head, piss on them, anything," Angelucci says. "One time, we were in the city jail and this cop saw him pass and said, 'Is that Gerry Gavin? Hold onto him.' He brought in eight other cops who stood in a gauntlet and made Gerry run through it as they punched and hit him. The whole time, Gerry was talking back, saying, 'I'll see you in the morning at breakfast!' When they took him away, I overheard police laughing about it, saying, 'Man, that kid can take a punch.'

"Eventually police figured out not to hold him anymore because he always flipped out in jail so much. They'd beat him up and afterward he'd yell at them from the cell, 'I didn't come in bleeding like this—what are they gonna say about that?' After a few hours, maybe after he passed out, they'd just kick him out of jail, rather than have to deal with any more paperwork on him."

In the booking photo, Constable Stan Joplin looks on as plainclothes police officer Mike Barnard holds Gavin's arm behind him. Gavin is noticeably bleeding from the mouth and is either laughing or snarling at the cameraman. Next

Constable Jim Parker (far left), stands with Rob Thacker, constable Gary Campbell (middle) and constable Esko Kajander (far right).
PHOTO: Vancouver Police Museum, N00582K

The H-Squad's John Flaten stands with a visibly nervous young offender.
PHOTO: Vancouver Police Museum, P02010

to him, Esko Kajander holds Gavin's wrist and hair back and is unexpectedly smiling at Gavin. "I'm laughing at Gerry in the photo because he was trying to be macho, saying this ridiculous stuff, and because his hair was over his eyes, I'm holding his hair back so the camera can see his face," recalls Kajander, who had arrested Gavin on previous occasions. "He was always one of the main characters in the gang, and everybody knew him."

There were others at the Fraser Street party that night who managed to escape arrest, including Gary Blackburn and Mac Ryan. "It was crazy, but we managed to get out of there. Heck, I think we even just made it to another party that night! There were a lot of nights that went that way," Ryan says.

The neighbourhood disturbance was given brief mention in the local newspapers. Approximately nineteen people had been arrested; bail was set at $250 for the men and $100 for the women. All were forced to sign statements swearing that they would be off the streets after nine o'clock at night. "The guys from *The Grape* got some money together and bailed the Clark Parkers out," recalls Bradley Bennett. The Youngbloods were apparently still trying to get the Clark Park gang to join the revolution. Angelucci and Gavin were held over the weekend until Monday; Williamson, although accused of creating a disturbance, a minor charge, was sent to Oakalla prison, as the Fraser Street incident was considered an infraction of his bail conditions.

Police attention was highly focused on the gang now. After the concert riots, with the "goon squad" on his tail and multiple arrests that summer, Mouse Williamson increasingly felt the pinch. Warnings had been issued from on high. Williamson's uncle, who occasionally lunched with a high-ranking police superintendent who cannot be named here, said that when the subject of the gang had come up, the officer apparently said, "Tell your fucking nephew and his friends that if they don't knock off that shit they've been doing, we're going to fucking kill them."

Commercial Drive has long had a spirit of activism and been the scene of countless political demonstrations in Vancouver. Recently, the Drive has seen May Day protests against capitalism and gentrification and demonstrations over natural gas pipeline expansion, and in the early 1950s, more than 1,000 people crammed into the Grandview Theatre to protest what residents considered the deterioration of the district. While there were neighbourhood res-

Constable Esko Kajander holds back Gerry Gavin for an arrest processing photo; Gavin smiles for the camera. Also pictured are Constable Stan Joplin (left) and Constable Mike Barnard (right). PHOTO: Vancouver Police Museum, N00582L

idents who had applauded the increased police presence near Clark Park that summer, many other residents bitterly organized against it.

On Saturday, July 15, 1972, an anti-police demonstration, billed as the Clark Park Freedom Rally, was held. Featuring angry speeches from East End neighbourhood residents and legal rights counsellors on hand to provide advice, the event had been advertised for two weeks in *The Grape*, and handbills and flyers for the event had covered notice boards and lampposts all over the area. An estimated 350 people, mostly youths, descended on the park that sunny afternoon to take in what organizers tried to frame as a block party, a festival-like gathering. At first glance, it hardly seemed to have the bitter rancour of an anti-establishment anti-police protest. Along with the free hot dogs and lemonade, live music was performed by local acts Crackers (billed as "a Clark Park area band"), the Lions Gate Jazz Band, and Sleepy John. The Clark Park baseball diamond finally got some legitimate use beyond acting as a battlefield for rumbles. One of the rally's events was an exhibition game put on by the

Kosmic League, an infamous amateur baseball team made up of artists, poets, and journalists, including local artist Gary Lee-Nova and future Canadian poet-laureate George Bowering. (Despite Bowering's keen memory, he does not recall any details of this particular game.)

The rally also attracted the attention of local media, with the *Sun*, *Province*, and *Georgia Straight* all on hand to report on the event. Their focus was not on

Clark Park Freedom Rally poster, July 1972.
SOURCE: Courtesy of the author

Chuck Reid addresses those gathered at the Clark Park Freedom Rally in July 1972. PHOTO: *Vancouver Sun*

music or baseball, but on the speeches protesting against police harassment, some given by parents of Clark Park gang members who felt their children had been subjects of police brutality. While it was believed at the time to be okay for parents to hit their own children, they were not going to allow the police to do so.

The most vocal of the speakers was Chuck Reid, a muscular forty-three-year-old electrician and father of three teenage children. Reid told the crowd: "I used to be scared about sending my kids out [on the street] because of rapists. Now I can't send them out without being scared of the police." He went on to say that his sons had been subject to hectoring and abusive language by police, who refused to identify themselves when requested. Reid did not openly admit to being anti-police; he insisted that he was "an establishment type" who had joined the protest because of his sons' experiences. He asked that anyone who had witnessed anything or wanted to file a complaint let him know about it as he had begun to keep records of the incidents, and gave out his home address near Trout Lake, just minutes away from Clark Park.[49]

Organizers listed a number of recorded police offences that had occurred in

49 Christy McCormick, "Clark Park Harassment: Peaceful Rally Raps Police Action," *Vancouver Sun*, July 17, 1972, 10.

recent weeks, many of which appeared to originate with the H-Squad. Specific dates when area youths were stopped for questioning immediately outside their homes or searched on the sidewalk were enumerated. On the back of the rally's flyer, organizers had written a half-true description of the Fraser Street incident, which stated that several dozen police had "broke up an up-til-then peaceful party," and failed to mention the original noise complaint or the bottles thrown at police.

Many in attendance were present just to take in the music and atmosphere and had not shown up with a political agenda. And despite the impassioned speeches, the event was, by all accounts, a very pleasant afternoon. Even when two police cars cruised by the park, at one point stopping to observe before they drove on, there was no incident. Although the Clark Park Freedom Rally had been open invitation, the H-Squad refrained from attending. "We figured some of our faces were already getting a little bit known around there," Stanton says.

Mac Ryan and Gary Blackburn, who attended the rally, recall seeing members of the Youngbloods there, as well as a group calling themselves the Volunteers who handed out a thirty-page handbook decorated with the black flag of anarchy, which explained the legal rights of Canadian citizens when dealing with the police. "[There] were these radical shitheads there who told us, 'You have rights. You don't have to tell police anything,'" recalls Blackburn. When he next encountered the H-Squad, he "yelled at them, saying, 'I've got rights, and you can't do this to me!' One of the squad just pulled me up to his face and said, 'You've got no fucking rights at all!' and threw me on the ground."

Not all present were in agreement with the organizers, including a Mr and Mrs Carlo Rigoni, a couple who lived across the street from the park. Speaking to a *Sun* reporter, Mrs Rigoni said she felt police were not being tough enough. "I'm afraid to use that park. I'm frightened that I'll get beaten or killed if I go there."[50] Despite Mrs Rigoni and a few others' voices of dissent, most in attendance—in particular those who were political activists—believed that the police were doing more harm than good, going after innocent adolescents.

At the rally, a petition was produced and circulated among the crowd for signatures, stating: "Specifically, we oppose the high level of unwarranted police intimidation and harassment, unnecessary police brutality and use of excessive

50 McCormick, 10.

force and the illegal use of off-duty and plainclothes police officers as vigilantes against young people in the Clark Park area of the city."[51] The rally raised questions not only about the police and what was happening in the East End, but about the gang itself. In a segment on the CBC television news, reporter Bill Dobson noted the concerns of rally organizers about "continued public attention focused on rowdyism and petty crime near Vancouver's neighbourhood parks." Dobson interviewed Mark Edelstein, an outreach worker with an East End youth centre called The Stay Project: "What about this discussion of gang problems at parks, and hassling by police?" he asked.

"There have been enough children coming here, enough words from parents, and what's in the newspapers to make us believe that there's certainly something happening around Clark Park," Edelstein said.

"Is it a gang problem, do you think?" Dobson asked.

"I think the gang is a myth."

"What about the police hassling?"

"That's not a myth. That's really happening. But from what we've heard its not the entire Vancouver police force hassling people in the area, but individual members of the force."[52]

The opinions of those who were on the Clark Park scene then haven't changed much. "They figured they were curing the problem—they just made it worse," says Rick Stuart. "What [the H-Squad] did was [bring] out a big hatred of cops in everybody in the neighbourhood, and that feeling stuck with people over the years. It did with me. They're the biggest fucking gang I've ever seen in my life."

Looking back, Gary Blackburn concurs. "They were supposed to intimidate—and they did to a point. They didn't stop anything from happening, but they probably made people start to watch their backs." And it made some want to fight back.

Just about everyone of a certain vintage who worked in the Vancouver Police Department has an Al Robson story or a favourite colourful anecdote of working with him. "I once went to answer a dispatch call at the Wings Hotel

51 Ibid.
52 CBC Television News, Untitled film strip, dated July 27, 1972 (Vancouver, BC: CBC Vancouver Archives).

The Wings Hotel, 1979.
PHOTO: City of Vancouver Archives, CVA 780-323

on Dunlevy off Gore Street," recalls Constable Chris Graham, who joined the department in the mid-1980s. "[I] was [on] a call [about] a man with a gun in the hotel, but not much was known beside that. I was on my own but was the only one nearby, so I radioed in that I'd take the call." Graham was a little nervous—he'd been in uniform for just a few months—when suddenly he overheard the voice of Robson, then a sergeant in another district, replying to the dispatcher, 'Tell that kid to wait there for me.'" Graham arrived at the hotel, and Robson screeched up in his patrol car a minute later. Stepping out of the car, he motioned to Graham and said, "All right, come with me." The two constables entered the hotel.

"We find out the guy had been shooting a gun off and yelling in his room," Graham says. "So Robson just pounds up the stairs down the hallway to his room, kicks open the door, grabs the gun out of the guy's hands, slaps him in the head, and tells him off. It turned out that the gun was a starter pistol and not really dangerous, but he couldn't have known that when he went in. I was stunned! When it was all over and we were leaving the hotel I asked him, 'How the hell'd you know it wasn't a real gun?' and Robson just grumbled and said everyone in the building were 'real assholes,' and that was it. But Robson did stuff like that every day. The younger guys completely idolized him."

Recalling the Wings Hotel incident in 2016, Al Robson says, "Well, I was at the end of my shift, and I didn't want to have to call in a barricade, close the street, bring in a negotiator, and have to write up all that paperwork. I just wanted to go for a drink after work."

With a brusque and happily unapologetic, politically incorrect sense of humour, Robson is the kind of headstrong, tough, no-bullshit policeman that today's generation of police academies can no longer produce. (Perhaps they never did.) Officers like Robson didn't have much sympathy for purse-snatching culprits who complained that their handcuffs were too tight after they'd just pushed an eighty-year-old woman to the ground. Surrounded by layers of official bureaucratic policy, sensitivity training, and passersby ready to pull out a camera phone to record an officer's every move, a man like Robson would find today's world of policing a difficult place in which to work. Yet he was ideal for his generation.

Born in Saskatchewan and raised in East Vancouver, Robson was the son of a policeman. He joined the VPD in 1971. His home neighbourhood would also become his first patrol. "Clark Park was my area—I was in car 311," he says. Clark Park was a known trouble-spot when he began as a police officer. "There were a bunch of houses along 14th at Commercial. The whole street was nothing but assholes."

Robson still recalls some of the neighbourhood problems that the Clark Park gang caused. "They were into a lot of burglaries, vandalism, mischief, and bullying. In those days, there wasn't much else to do," he says half-jokingly. "At one time, around 18th and Commercial, the city had run a gas line and dug a trench in the street, four-and-a-half feet wide and two feet deep. They put up a sawhorse with flashing hazard signs, but these little bastards had taken them away, and a couple of people had driven into the ditch at night. One lady drove through the unmarked road, buried her face right through the windshield of her Toyota, and got hurt pretty bad. I got interviewed by the city in the investigation and insurance claim by the woman. Nobody was ever caught for it, but we all knew it was them."

On September 16, 1972, Robson and Constable Ted (Ed) McClellan had just sat down on a break and ordered dinner at the White Spot restaurant at Gladstone Street and Kingsway when their police radio squawked a disturbance call: "Two men fighting on Sidney Street," just a few blocks away. Robson and McClellan jumped into their patrol car and drove to the location where they spotted a couple of young men fighting on the road as they pulled up. "When I opened the door, they both suddenly ran up and bashed the door on my leg. When I got the door open, four more jumped over a fence and came after us. That's when we knew it was a set-up."

Policemen injured by street rowdies

Two police officers required hospital treatment for injuries received Saturday in a battle with an east end gang that ended with three arrests.

Const. A. D. Robson received hand and leg injuries when the door of his police car was slammed against him as he was attempting to leave the vehicle.

Const. Ed. McClellan was kicked in the head, suffered facial injuries and a hairline skull fracture. Robson was released from hospital following treatment. McClellan was kept under observation for about 12 hours before being discharged.

Charged with assaulting the two officers and causing a disturbance are: Randolph George Johnston, 18, Terry Reid, 17, and a 16-year-old juvenile. Johnston and Reid were released Sunday on their undertaking to appear in provincial court Tuesday.

Johnston also faces a charge of possession of a dangerous weapon — a length of dog chain with a lead weight tied to one end.

Police say they believe the eight youths involved in the street fight were members of what is known as the Clark Park Gang. Five of the youths fled when the police officers called for reinforcements.

In the summer of 1972, police and the Clark Park gang went to war.
SOURCE: *The Province.*

As another two men also jumped out, Robson recalls that McClellan was hit hard in the head and went down. "I was pretty big in those days, and I grabbed three of them and hit them all hard, handcuffing one of them and hanging him over the branch of a tree." Robson then yelled for backup over the radio, and several of the men ran off. "It took a long time for backup to get there—they weren't near."

The incident was reported in *The Province*, which called it "a street battle with an east end gang" and noted that it "ended with three arrests." McClellan had suffered a hairline skull fracture and spent the night in hospital. While a number of the young men in the fight escaped, *The Province* reported that "Randolph George Johnston, eighteen, Terry Reid, seventeen, and a sixteen-year-old juvenile" were arrested. Johnston faced a charge of possession of a dangerous weapon, "a length of dog chain with a lead weight tied to one end." The article also noted: "Police say they believe the eight youths involved in the street fight were members of what is known as the Clark Park Gang."[53]

That Clark Park gang members were armed with weapons was not a new development. Weapons had always been seen at rumbles, and rumours had it that the gang had hidden caches in Clark Park itself. Constable Paul Stanton notes, "We never found any weapons in the park, but I wouldn't have been surprised if they had some in there." Most Clark Parkers claim that while some individuals might have stashed items in the park, this was just another one of the dark rumours that followed the gang.

The newspaper article didn't tell the complete story, however. Johnston's dog chain, hidden in his boot, was found only after he'd been arrested and used it in another fight in the holding cell that evening. Robson, recalling the fight in 2016, remembers, "I'd hit Johnston pretty hard after Ted [McClellan] got hit. Ted was knocked out so hard, he was muttering for his wife and thought he was at a bowling tournament in Las Vegas ... I had hit Terry Reid hard enough that he was still on the ground when Ted managed to get up, and he kicked Reid. Just then, Chuck Reid showed up. It turned out Terry was his kid—and they both wanted to press charges for assault." Although Terry Reid and others had initiated the assault, Reid's father stood by his son.

The Reids would have their day in court: Constable McClellan was charged with assault. On the day of the hearing to set a trial date, Al Robson stood outside the courtroom waiting for his partner when the doors opened. "Ted came out, and then Chuck Reid with his kid after him," Robson says. "Before he left, Chuck pointed at Ted and said, 'You better watch your back!'" With plenty of witnesses on hand, Chuck Reid was subsequently charged with ut-

53 "Policemen Injured by Street Rowdies," *The Province*, September 18, 1972, 23.

tering threats. Eventually, the judge and prosecutor arranged for a settlement: both the assault charge against McClellan and the charge against Chuck Reid were dismissed.

The street fight between police and the gang remains one of the more public examples of the nature of the relationship between the two groups that summer. Members of the Clark Park gang were now staging incidents to draw police into direct confrontation, and some gang members spoke of getting into fights with police as an evening's entertainment. (Efforts to reach Terry Reid through other old associates of the Clark Park gang for comment were not fruitful.)

For the most part, however, it was a peaceful summer in the city. Besides the Rolling Stones riot, Vancouver had avoided a major public clash like the Gastown riot or the Sea Festival incidents. But there was still noticeable tension, an as yet unlit powder-keg of distrust between young people and the police. In a *Vancouver Sun* article, reporter Keith Taylor canvassed 500 Vancouver youths and found that young people in Vancouver believed the treatment that citizens could expect at the hands of police depended on how old they were and how they were dressed. "Don't let the uneasy truce fool you," wrote Taylor. "Unless the two sides can get together to try to understand each other, to become more aware of each other's thinking, the peace will never last—and the violence with all its attendant ugliness will flare up again in our city."[54]

Taylor, of course, was unaware that a secret war between the H-Squad and the Clark Park gang was already being waged. While the Sidney Street fight was mentioned in the newspapers, other incidents remained classified. One weekend that summer, during an evening sweep of East Vancouver, police arrested nine Clark Parkers, who were brought to the Main Street police lockup. Among those arrested were Mouse Williamson, Rod Schnob, Dwayne Nelson, and Larry Booth.

"When we were at the booking desk, one of the guards in the jail started to rough up Rod," Williamson recounts. "Rod pushed back and yelled, 'You guys are all gutless pricks. You'd never go one on one!' The guard who was dealing with him barked, 'Yeah, I would!' and some of the other guards at the desk said they would too. Rod and this cop just start to fight right there. Another

54 Alan Daniels, "Young People Complain: The Police Discriminate Against Us," *Vancouver Sun*, October 5, 1972, 6.

cop went to jump on Rod, and Larry Booth jumped in to hold that cop back. While those two started to square off, another cop tried to jump on Larry, and Dwayne Nelson jumped on him. The rest of us tried to pin the other cops back, yelling, 'You said a fair fight, one on one!'"

There, in the middle of the police booking room, an impromptu bare-knuckle fight broke out. The Clark Parkers egged on their comrades while police cheered their fellow officers as the lockup roared with obscenities and desks were noisily pushed out of the way. According to Williamson, Schnob began to get the better of the guard he was fighting, and all the men voluntarily broke it up. The gang insisted they'd won the match as they were hustled to their cells.

Booking Desk at 312 Main Street Police Station, c. 1970s.
PHOTO: Vancouver Police Museum, P00156

Did police have a different judgement of the fight's outcome, and can they even verify that it took place? The incident was never leaked to media at the time, and if there are any police still living who recall the incident, none are talking. That no police officer simply pulled out his firearm to stop the fight is difficult to believe, but Williamson insists that the story is not a fabrication. If police had come to despise the Clark Parkers just as much as the Clark Parkers hated them, perhaps they shared an appetite for brawls. "Everything happened so fast," says Williamson. "I doubt that anything like it ever happened again ...

The cops just don't play that way. If they did have security cameras in the jail, I bet they erased the tapes pretty quick, and I wouldn't be the least bit surprised if they all got together afterward and said, 'Don't mention this to anyone.'"

With the Clark Parkers in their cells and the lockup cleaned up after the melee, Williamson recalls what happened next. "After the fight, when things had calmed down, they pulled Rod [Schnob] aside and said, 'Hey, why don't you come work with us? We could use a guy with good hands like you. You should join the force,' but Rod told them to fuck off." Would Schnob have made a decent policeman? We'll never know. In 1984, he was arrested and convicted as a hitman in a sensational contract killing of a drug dealer in the small town of Duncan, BC. The hit went awry; the drug dealer's wife was murdered instead. Schnob received a minimum twenty-five-year life sentence.

NINE: STREET FIGHTIN' MAN

Throughout the fall of 1972, in the wake of the Sidney Street fight, rumours swirled that the Clark Park gang still planned to lure a uniformed patrol officer to a staged incident, perhaps even in the park itself, and attack him. But it's difficult to know, some forty-five years later, if the rumour had any substance. Former gang member Bradley Bennett has doubts. "We had no organization. If something did happen, it was completely by chance and spur of the moment. It was, 'Let's get stoned and drunk and go somewhere,' and then all of a sudden all fucking hell would break loose," he says. The disorganization of the gang made it difficult for police to predict where they would next show up to cause a problem. Individual Clark Parkers had their own agendas; each was considered by police to be as much of a problem as the next.

Mac Ryan recalls learning that another Clark Parker, Danny Teece, had been stopped by the squad that summer. "They ... accused him of being one of the fire bombers at the Stones concert, took out these knives, and slashed up a brand-new vest he was wearing." Ryan says the police threatened Teece the next time they saw him, saying they would cut up more than his vest. As a teen, Teece had fallen in with Paul Melo and another gang member, Robert "Bum" Wadsworth; in 1969, they were arrested for three B and Es and for the theft of a car. Teece's divorced parents then decided that he would be better off away from Clark Park and sent him to attend school in Maple Ridge, outside the city, where his grandmother lived. But Teece didn't like it there and moved back into town. He quit school in the spring of 1972, worked a few legitimate jobs here and there, spent weeks away from home, and ran around town with Clark Park friends. "Danny Teece was my good little buddy," says Wayne Angelucci. "We used to hang around all the time. He was younger than us, and we got into all kinds of crazy trouble—but he was a good kid. Everybody liked Danny, and he was easy to get along with."

If the H-Squad's surveillance and other activities were beginning to cause stress within the gang, it was difficult to determine. They were already leading complicated lives that, even without extra pressure, could at any moment lead to random violence. Even having a Clark Parker as a neighbour could invite trouble. Mac Ryan lived in an apartment with a friend from Clark Park for a while, and while Ryan hadn't been a keen student, he was an avid reader—he even subscribed to a daily newspaper. After staying up late one night drinking with friends, he woke up in the morning a little worse for wear and went to pick up the newspaper that was usually right outside his apartment door—but this time, it wasn't there.

Mac Ryan, 1970s.
PHOTO: Courtesy of Danny Williamson

"There were these college guys who lived in the apartment across the hall, and I got it in my head that they must have taken my newspaper," he says. Ryan pounded on their door. When one of them opened it, he barged in and demanded the return of the stolen newspaper. The two students, along with two visiting friends, told him that they didn't have it. Ryan accused them of lying, of taking him for a fool, and summoned his roommate. The two men punched up the college students in their own living room and stormed back across the hall, still angered that the neighbours would so blatantly steal the paper.

"I realized when I woke up the next day that it had actually been a holiday and there wasn't a newspaper delivery that day," he says. "I went over to apologize, but they'd packed up and moved out. Scared, I guess. I felt pretty bad about that one."

If Gerry Gavin was worried about the H-Squad, it didn't show, though Gavin was unpredictable. "If you were Gerry's friend, you were fine. But Gerry had a dark side to him, and he could turn on people," says Bradley Bennett. Bennett recalls one night when a group of Clark Parkers were at a party at Gary Blackburn's house. Mac Ryan's mother showed up with a new boyfriend and his younger brother, who was closer in age to the gang. "They dumped him

Bradley Bennett and Mouse Williamson. c. 1970s.
PHOTO: Courtesy of Bradley Bennett

off at the party while they went out. He didn't know anybody, and he didn't fit in at all. He was trying, but most guys just ignored him. Gerry Gavin instantly hated him, and so he beat him up really bad. Gerry even went to grab a claw hammer to beat him with, but we pulled him off."

When Mac's mother and her boyfriend returned, they found the younger brother passed out in the living room with two swollen eyes and a cut lip; his face was covered in bruises. The boyfriend demanded to know what had happened to him, but party-goers sheepishly said that they had no idea. "He was a big guy, and he could have individually beaten all of us up, one at a time, I'm sure," Bennett says. "He grabbed somebody and was going to hit him if he didn't say who had beaten up his brother. Then Gerry piped up: 'Hey, I'm the one who beat him up—and I'm going to beat you.'" The men charged at each other, but others stepped in to break up the fight, kicking the older brother out of the party. He left, taking his unconscious sibling with him out to the car, and drove off. "Mac's mother stayed behind with us and drank. She said to us, 'He was a nice guy who treated me well—why do you do that to all my boyfriends?'" Bennett says. "It hadn't been the first time."

Bradley Bennett and Mouse Williamson were out with a number of others from the gang one afternoon in Grandview Park when police spotted and detained them. "They used to make you take your jacket off, and they'd write down what tattoos you had. This was long before cell phone cameras, of course, and I guess they were too cheap to get a Polaroid, but they kept these little cards on everybody and asked us our names as they went through it," says Bennett. "They hassled us for about ten or fifteen minutes and finally let us go. Somebody said, 'Hey, Mouse, let's get the fuck out of here,' and as soon as the cops heard that, they grabbed him again. The beat cops only knew him as Danny and didn't realize he was 'Mouse.' They'd been looking for a 'Mouse' for years, but never knew his real name. Hell, I never knew his real name either! I'd only ever known him as 'Mouse,' but the cops knew him only from his ID."

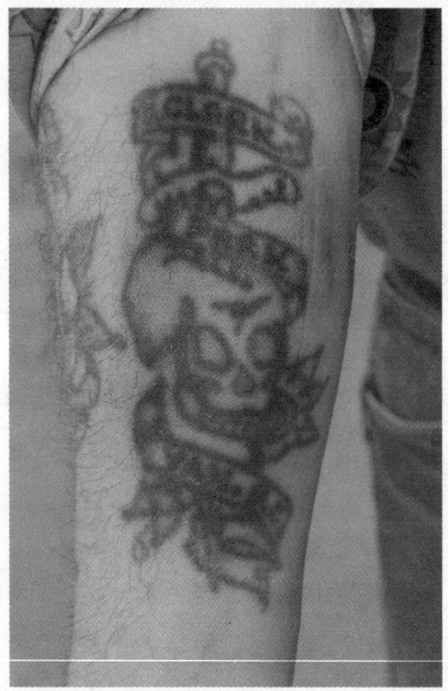
Mouse Williamson got his Clark Park tattoo in the early 1970s. PHOTO: Erik Iversen, 2016

At the end of August, Williamson finally went to court for the charge of assaulting an officer at the Rolling Stones riot the year before. He was found guilty, although he said that he was unaware his victim was a police officer. If Williamson already had reasons to be angry about the conviction, it got worse when his sentencing hearing was held. Ken Doern (Bell) testified that he'd seen Williamson with a gun at his house. The judge believed Doern's testimony, and Williamson was given a two-year sentence in Oakalla prison. Williamson was furious—as far as he was concerned, Doern had lied. "I saw him years later and asked him why he had lied. He sheepishly said he couldn't remember or would have to check his notes. But it was all bullshit. I bet he was padding all his undercover reports this way to make it look like he was getting all this good information."

In a strange way, Williamson's sentence came as welcome relief. "Between the Fraser Street party and my court case, I'd been out of jail for twenty-eight days, and I was never so happy to go back in. Every time I was out on the street, the [H-Squad] cops would stop me, insult me, slap me around. I couldn't go anywhere."

Clark Parkers were being taken off the street. Williamson was now in jail, Mark

Owens was doing a year for armed robbery, and Bradley Bennett was also in prison again, this time on a conviction for assaulting a police officer. Those on the outside were getting older or just busier, and began to drift away from the park scene. There were only so many houses in the East End they could break into. Eventually, some considered more legitimate forms of work. "By 1972, I started to work on the tugboats with my father. I was attracted to the idea of working on the water," says Rick Stuart. "I'd be gone for weeks at a time. It was nice to not be so broke. I'd come back and see everybody [in the gang] and end up getting into a little trouble, but I'd quickly be back out on the boats again."

Another Clark Parker who had begun to move on was Wayne Angelucci. "I didn't hang around the park as much when I got older," he says. "I thought it was a waste of time. The only time I stayed out of trouble was when I'd be in jail—three months here, three months there. Mac and I were both in, doing time together. But I wanted to have money. There used to be logging companies that had labour offices on Hastings Street, so I went down to Pigeon Park, got a haircut, and went to one office. The guy said, 'There's a plane leaving for the logging camp in Tahsis in two hours. I can put you on that.' So I went to work up at the logging camps, and that got me out of the park for a month or so at a time. They phoned my father and let him know where I was, and asked if it was okay with him, because I was so young, but I'd quit school and wasn't doing anything else. So I'd work, then come back to town and see everybody and spend all my money, and then go back up [north] and do it again." Although some Clark Parkers were now off the streets or at least spent less time there, the H-Squad continued to go after the remaining gang members in the East End.

Police cars in the neighbourhood were continually made to feel unwelcome. "They were breaking a lot of windows in the backs of patrol cars," remembers Constable Paul Stanton, especially if they were unattended at various trouble spots throughout East Van. The gang continued to invite conflict with the police that summer, sometimes for seemingly harmless things—at least in comparison to other crimes they'd been involved in—but police took them just as seriously.

"Somebody stole a policeman's hat out of the back of a patrol car. The cops went nuts over that; it was a big insult to them," says Gary Blackburn. "When I heard about it, I felt bad about that one, because the particular cop was a really nice guy. He'd come by the park and tell us, 'Get the fuck out of here because there are people coming up to get you guys.' He treated us decently. I mean, if we'd done something wrong or got busted for something fair and square, no problem, he'd arrest you for it, but he treated us fairly. I guess he'd taken his hat off and thrown it in the back of the car, so it got stolen. That hat got passed around the entire East End. People took pictures of them wearing it on their heads at parties, and it was a couple of years before it was found again." But more significant burglaries took place as well, and that summer the gang's criminal activities did not slow down.

The railyards were always a favourite target for robberies. The long boxcars were difficult to guard at night and made for easy scores. "A few of the guys broke into a boxcar. It was full of Winchester rifles. There was no ammunition with them, but the police went nuts, thinking that we were now all armed with guns," says Gary Blackburn. He believes now that most of the guns were later recovered when they were found scattered and discarded.

The railyard thefts would not always yield such a bounty. On another occasion, the gang broke into a boxcar hoping there would be television sets or some other high-value items inside, but it was full of boxes of Cap'n Crunch cereal. "The next day, one of the newspapers, covering our great train robbery, ran a headline: 'Hoodlums Munch on Cap'n Crunch,'" Williamson recalls with a laugh.

Most of the gang's burglaries were more profitable, usually yielding cash or items of value that could easily be sold or stored in neighbourhood garages. Police rarely caught the thieves in the act. But one night, Mac Ryan and other gang members stole some lawnmowers and gardening equipment. With the gear loaded onto the back of a flatbed owned by one of the gang, they made a clean getaway. But as they drove back into the East End with the haul, they were pulled over by a passing police car. "It was late at night, and the cop asked us what we were doing with all the stuff," Ryan says. "We told him it was equipment for a landscaping job we had the next day, and we were just going to drop the gear off at job site to get a head start. He looked at it, and then he looked at us. He knew us from Clark Park. He said, 'I know who all of you are, and if I read a report tomorrow that somebody woke up and found their lawnmowers stolen, I'm coming around to pick every one of you up and arrest you.'" They protested, with Ryan even telling the police that he was offended that such assumptions would be made. They assured the officer that the gear was all equipment for the next day's work, so the police let them go on their way. Knowing they'd already been caught, however, they had to drive all the gear back and reluctantly—and quietly—return it.

The H-Squad was not without its own unexpectedly humorous incidents. Squad member Jim Maitland recalls that one night he, Joe Cliffe, and John Flaten were doing a surveillance of the park to see if any gang members had shown up. Needing to make a personal call at a pay phone, Flaten stepped away and walked down Commercial Drive after agreeing to meet up with the other officers later in a different corner of the park. Cliffe sat in one car, while Maitland drove to 16th and Commercial to wait. Just then, they heard some noises and suspected that something was up.

"Some time went by," Maitland recalls, "and Flaten came back on the radio and asked, 'Where are you guys?' We told him, and he said he was going to go into Clark Park alone and meet us at our corner. So we wait a couple of minutes when all of a sudden we hear this screaming coming from inside the park. We jumped out of our cars and ran up, and there was Flaten with a guy in each hand, holding them upside down. He'd apparently come out of nowhere and grabbed them. They must've thought they'd been attacked by a grizzly bear. It turns out they weren't Clark Park gang people but a couple of young university students. Their parents didn't like them drinking in their house, so they thought they'd grab a six-pack and drink it in the park. They were having a good time when Flaten grabbed them."

The officers apologized and explained that they were police on a stakeout, and that it was a case of mistaken identity. "[The students] apologized profusely for drinking in public, but once we explained things to them, they took it in stride and were fine. But they were initially so scared that they probably never went into Clark Park again. Heck, after meeting Big John in the dark like that, I wouldn't be surprised if they never drank again."

By the fall of 1972, concerns were raised within the Vancouver Police Department administration that the continued activities of the H-Squad—and its very existence—were becoming an issue. "I got the feeling that the department was just starting to get too much heat over us," says Constable Paul Stanton. It's unknown how many complaints were filed against police that summer, but none were delivered to Joe Cliffe, the leader of the H-Squad; the sensitive nature of their existence meant that complaints went straight to police superintendents who either appeared to delay acting on them or perhaps ignored them altogether.

Undercover surveillance revealed that Chuck Reid, various Clark Parkers, and some other local activists were seen meeting in the Gastown law office of Harry Rankin, the city's legendary (and volatile) activist lawyer and noted alderman. Stanton believes they consulted with him for legal advice. Rankin had earned a reputation as a lawyer who was not shy about going after the police. He fought the case on behalf of Fred Quilt, an Aboriginal man who had allegedly died of mistreatment in 1971 at the hands of the RCMP. The possibility of Rankin's involvement might have been almost enough on its own to halt the squad's operations.

While Harry Rankin's focus on the Vancouver Police Department was of concern, as were public complaints to the VPD, the results of that summer's provincial election also helped to spell the end of the H-Squad. In the August vote, the left-leaning BC New Democratic Party (NDP) under Dave Barrett had beaten the right-wing Social Credit government. Attorney General Leslie Peterson was turfed out of office, and NDP appointee Alex MacDonald was in. While Peterson had apparently been made aware of the H-Squad and given it his approval, the VPD might have believed MacDonald would not have equally approved of the H-Squad's tactics.

Complaints about police had increased in the East End, but the force also enjoyed the support of residents in the neighbourhood around the park. Constable Howard Corbett recalls being at the police station one afternoon when a mother brought in her son and said she wanted to file a complaint. "I overheard her yelling in the superintendent's office—not about police, but about her son," Corbett says. "She kept saying that he was a little shit and thief and hoodlum, and that other than being slapped upside the head, he wasn't injured. She said that he had deserved some discipline for once."

On the streets and around the park, local residents were tiring of the frequent burglaries, bullying, and unending disturbances and hellraising that the gang brought to the park. While it's certain some complaints about the H-Squad's actions were brushed aside or not acted upon, some neighbours were pleased that there was finally a little peace in the neighbourhood. Today, some would state that the alleged rough tactics that the H-Squad employed were just as illegal as the methods used by gang members themselves. Others might welcome such an aggressive police attitude, and that the gangs were finally being dealt with so firmly. Whether for good or not, these were the unorthodox means to an end that Vancouver police used in the early 1970s when other strategies had failed to achieve results.

In October of 1972, the H-Squad was officially disbanded; its members moved on to other departments with commendations. By and large, police believed that the squad's tactics had worked—the gang no longer hung around in the park, and some key members had been put in jail. Police felt like they'd won and broke up the Clark Park network.

While the police had made an impact, time made another. The gang was no longer hanging out in the parks, in part because many of them were now old enough to be admitted into east side pubs and bars. Riley Parkers and Clark Parkers seated at different tables on opposite sides of the room eventually, slowly, got to know one another. While they may have fought at times, they'd likely seen each other from days going back to juvenile detention, and while it didn't happen overnight, in the bars they now began to socialize. The East Enders didn't tend to go to downtown nightclubs, dinner and dance cabarets, or show lounges—greasers in mack jackets and jeans were not welcome in those upscale establishments. The park gang crowds instead frequented the hotel beer parlours and biker pubs in East Vancouver—the Eldorado Hotel, the Blue Boy, Lasseter's Den—or headed to last call at the Biltmore.

TEN: A SHOT IN THE DARK

At 4:30 a.m. on November 25, 1972, a man named Kirk Brennan reported to the police that his 1964 light-blue Chevrolet convertible had been stolen from outside his home in East Vancouver. Later that night, a Mrs L. Matheson, who resided in southeast Vancouver, reported that her Admiral TV had been stolen from her home sometime between November 24 and November 28 when she'd been away. Neither robbery appeared remarkable—they were typical of the auto or property theft calls filed every day with city police. In 1967, police had responded to 40,000 calls—reports of crimes ranging from murders to fender-benders—and that number would double by 1972.[55] No one would have guessed, looking at these mundane and seemingly unrelated thefts, that they would set into motion a series of events resulting in tragic circumstances, the consequences of which are still in the minds of some East Vancouverites today.

The 1968 Chevy convertible stolen by members of the Clark Park gang.
PHOTO: Vancouver Police Department, 72-64202_2

55 "Stokes Recalls the Days of Street Justice," *Vancouver Sun*, October 7, 1975, 21.

"I can't remember how we found the car," says Gary Blackburn. "We stole so many of the damn things back then, sometimes three or four a day. But that was the big thing back then—you'd steal a car and then break into a house and grab a TV." Blackburn, along with Paul Melo, Danny Teece, and another Clark Parker, Robert "Bum" Wadsworth, were all involved in both the car and TV theft that night.

Wadsworth had escaped from Haney Correctional Institute earlier that summer where he'd been serving a two-years-less-a day sentence for a conviction on eighteen charges, varying from breaking and entering to stolen property to auto theft. He knew the other three men from stays in the juvenile detention home and other burglaries. "East Van was a tough neighbourhood," says Wadsworth, thinking back on his adolescence four decades earlier. "The gangs hide out now, but everybody was out on the street back then." Today, Wadsworth lives near the downtown eastside and is quiet and taciturn, leaving the impression that life over the years has not always been easy for him. Mac Ryan recalls how he got his nickname: "The hersheys [gang slang for upper-class collegiate types] back then would say something good was 'mint.' We called the opposite of that 'bummy,' so we'd called him 'Bum.'"

Paul Melo would later admit to authorities that he stole the car while drunk when he was by himself on November 25. Cars back then, especially Chevrolets, were relatively easy to steal; the ignition could be turned on without a key. While they could be stolen by a single person, television sets in the 1970s were large floor units, more like pieces of furniture and as heavy as some appliances, and often needed two or three people to lift and carry. The four men recall little about the TV they stole on November 27 from Mrs Matheson's home at around 6:30 p.m. that day. That kind of break-and-enter was simply too frequent an occurrence to fully recall.

After they stole the TV, they put it in the Chevrolet and drove closer to the Biltmore Hotel pub, randomly choosing the underground lot of a small residential apartment building at 310 East 14th, just off Sophia Street, to park it. The apartment building, still there today, is situated in the quiet neighbourhood of Mount Pleasant. Although Main Street has evolved beyond recognition since the 1970s, the surrounding residential streets remain relatively unchanged, and are still lined with two- and three-storey apartment buildings built in the mid- to late 1960s.

Entrance to the underground parking lot behind 310 East 14th Avenue.
PHOTO: Vancouver Police Department, 72-6402_16

The underground parking lot leading up to the alley behind East 14th and Sophia Street.
PHOTO: Vancouver Police Department, 72-6402_14

The thieves left the car in an empty parking stall, then walked three blocks north to the Biltmore to see if they could find a buyer for the television. As they walked, Blackburn remembers thinking that nothing was out of the ordinary and that the underground lot was a good spot for the car; it wasn't likely to be seen, especially at that time of the evening. He figured they'd be at the bar for no more than a couple of hours. The four men entered the Biltmore at about 8:30 p.m., where they bumped into two other Clark Parkers, Rob Thacker and Doug Louacki, who were drinking and playing pool.

Today the Biltmore is a live-music club, especially popular with young millennial crowds, and hosts bands, DJs, comedy nights, and burlesque. But in the early 1970s, its underground, low-ceilinged, smoky atmosphere lent it a dark sleaziness, and a rough East End clientele was known to frequent it.

The Biltmore Hotel in 1963.
PHOTO: Grant-Mann Lithographers, Vancouver, C-1203

Over a few beers, the men scanned the bar as people came in and went out, checking for faces they'd recognize who might be interested in the stolen TV. But Gary Blackburn remembers sensing that something wasn't right. They hadn't been ID'd when they came in. He was still seventeen and looked young, and Teece, who was also seventeen, looked even younger. "I thought it was weird that we got in ... We weren't just hanging around in a corner either; we were there for a couple of hours, using the pay phone to call around. I knew a guy who bought TVs, and I finally got hold of him. Once we made the arrangements, we finished our beers just before midnight, and made our way out to drive over to him." It all seemed straightforward—they'd hand over the TV, collect their money, and divide it up before they headed home.

While Blackburn, Teece, Melo, and Wadsworth were at the Biltmore, the caretaker who lived in the building where they'd parked the car was busy reading out the license plate to a police dispatcher. He'd spotted the four men earlier, who were unfamiliar to him and looked suspicious as they left the underground lot. And when he went down to check on the parking area, he found the car that didn't belong there. At approximately 9:30 p.m., two plainclothes officers were dispatched to check things out on the report of a possible stolen vehicle. In the patrol car was Constable Esko Kajander. Since the Fraser Street incident in June, Kajander, still working out of the District, had been posted to plainclothes duty. That night, he was working the evening shift with his senior partner Ian Battcock, who had joined the police department in 1965.

The officers parked their unmarked car, and Kajander walked west down the lane. He went into the underground parking lot, saw the vehicle, confirmed the license plate, and spoke to the building manager. Kajander confirmed that the car had been reported as stolen; the officers radioed back to dispatch that it was the car belonging to Kirk Brennan and noted that a TV set was in the back seat. "What you did back then was sit on things and wait to see if anything would happen," says Kajander, adding that had the stolen vehicle been found without the TV, it might have been towed to the police impound, but the TV made police suspect that the thieves would return shortly.

Another patrol car was sent to assist Battcock and Kajander, carrying constables Brian Honeybourn and Bruce Campbell, who were also on plainclothes duty. A plan was made to wait until the thieves returned; once they drove the car out, the police would try to block them in the alleyway. The constables split up into pairs; Honeybourn and Campbell parked at the eastern end of the alleyway in front of Mount Saint Joseph Hospital on Prince Edward Street, and Kajander and Battcock parked at the west end of the alley on Sophia Street, closer to the entrance of the underground parking lot. At opposite ends of the alley, the men kept in contact via police radio—and waited.

"I thought that whoever had stolen the car was probably in the Biltmore, probably looking to sell the TV," Honeybourn recalls. "We all knew that the

Biltmore was a rough place then, and fencing stolen stuff wouldn't have been out of the ordinary there."

Police surveillance can be a mundane task. There are no set rules or traditions, though some insist that the last cop to arrive on location has to bring the coffee and rolls. Depending on the relationship with one's partner, there's all manner of small talk exchanged while sitting in a car—inter-office police gossip, local sports highlights, or jokes—to cut the boredom. Sometimes there is just silence, watching, and waiting. Time slows down in those moments. You can only look at your wristwatch so many times.

Police investigation PHOTOgraph of the alleyway off East 14th Avenue.
PHOTO: Vancouver Police Department, 72-6402_4

After a while, they half-expected to be ordered away by dispatch to deal with another incident, but it was a quiet evening, and no other emergency calls came through. More than an hour went by. Battcock wanted to call off the surveillance and radio for a tow truck to take the vehicle to police impound, but the officers decided to wait a little longer.

Eventually, Campbell got out of the car to have a look around. He had wandered down the alleyway when he heard a short tap of the horn from

Honeybourn, so he ran back to their car. Honeybourn had heard from Kajander that four men were coming down Sophia Street and heading into the alley.

It was about ten minutes after midnight when Blackburn, Teece, Melo, and Wadsworth walked back to the stolen car. "I sort of had a feeling the cops had staked it out," Wadsworth recalls. "Before we went underground to get the car, I said something, but the others said to forget about it." The air felt prickly to Gary Blackburn too. "Something didn't feel right. I'd had those feelings before, but I just didn't listen to my senses that night."

Wadsworth stayed on the street at the entry of the parkade to keep an eye out while the other three went to the car. They tried to cover up the TV with a blanket—four scruffy young males driving a good convertible around at that hour of the night with a large TV in the back seat would draw attention. But before they got into the car, Blackburn and Teece flipped a coin to see who would take the back seat. "We always switched up so we'd all get a chance to drive, and it was Paul's turn. [The Chevrolet] was a two-door; you had to push the front seat forward to get into and out of the back. It was up to me and Danny [Teece] as to which of us would sit in the back seat]. I lost the flip and had to get in the back with the TV. Up front, Danny sat in the middle."

Several minutes after police had seen the men enter the underground lot, a light above the entranceway suddenly flickered and went out. It was difficult to tell in the darkness if someone had removed it or it had simply burned out—but it increased the tension for the police. Then headlights appeared, and Battcock and Kajander saw the Chevrolet quietly glide out of the dark and up the ramp where the man acting as a lookout got in.

Kajander and Battcock radioed to Honeybourn and Campbell that the car had exited the lot and was headed down the alley in their direction. After a moment, in order to give the Chevrolet a short head start, Battcock turned into the alley to follow the car. At the other end, Campbell waited until the Chevrolet had almost reached them at Prince Edward Street to turn on the flashing lights, put the car in drive, and quickly turn into the lane.

In the back seat, Gary Blackburn noticed the police car's lights in the grill of the unmarked car behind them. "I turned back, someone said, 'Police!' and there was another car coming right at us," Blackburn says. The doors to the Chevrolet flew open. "Everybody jumped out while the car was still moving.

Paul and Bob got out of the front seat, but for me to get out of the back, I had to push the seat forward. I was third out of the car, and Danny was the last as he came out behind me."

The Chevrolet slowed and hit the front bumper of Honeybourn and Campbell's car. Honeybourn jumped from the passenger side. Campbell quickly threw the police car in park, leapt from the driver's side, and shouted, "Police, stay where you are!" He saw the thieves flee toward the adjacent carport at the back of Prince Edward Manor, a three-storey apartment building at 3075 Prince Edward Street. As Campbell shouted, he drew his gun from his hip holster and started to chase the men.

It had rained in Vancouver in the two days before. Vancouver's rainy season tends to be in full-swing in the month of November. There are dozens of wet-weather days in any given November in the city, but this one proved particularly unfortunate. It was almost as if the rain had left the roads, sidewalks, and alleyways just wet enough to conspire with Campbell's decision to take out his gun, because as he chased the thieves, he slipped and lost his footing, and that's when the gun went off.

It was the first time in his seven years with the police department that Campbell had fired his gun on the job. "Just as I got out of the front of the car ... a shot went off near my ear," says Brian Honeybourn. "I was about fifteen feet away from Bruce. I saw the flash, and I saw him go down." Thinking that Campbell had been hit, Honeybourn took out his gun. Kajander and Battcock also heard the shot but kept chasing after the men running into the carport. It was dark, so they couldn't determine the ages of those running, though Battcock thought they looked like young men in their late teens.

On the second storey of the Prince Edward Manor, Richard Underwood was just getting into bed when he heard what sounded like a group of people running below his window—and then he heard the first shot. Underwood had experience with guns and hunting rifles and knew the different sounds certain firearms make. He immediately recognized the sound of a small-calibre policeman's pistol. Looking out the window, he saw the flashing police lights and heard his neighbour on the floor above him shout, "There's a kid running across the street there!"

Fifteen-year-old Dorothy Bridgman had just gone to bed in the third-storey suite above Underwood's when she heard someone yelling "Halt!" or

Police photo at the location of the Danny Teece shooting.
PHOTO: Vancouver Police Department, 72-6402_6

"Stop!" Then she heard a shot, which also woke her mother, and they both got out of their beds.

When he heard the first shot, "I thought, *These crazy fuckers are shooting at us*," says Gary Blackburn. He'd heard similar shots before when police, on raids in Clark Park, had fired warning shots, but says that, "anytime you heard that, you just wanted to run faster. I had no doubt they were shooting directly at us."

Melo and Wadsworth had already climbed over a concrete block wall between two apartment buildings, and Blackburn made it over next. "My heart was racing so fast, and once I got over, I ran to the other side of the street," says Blackburn.

Battcock was trailing after Kajander as they ran into the carport. Danny Teece was halfway over the wall when Brian Honeybourn reached him. "I got hold of him by the scruff before he went over and tried to drag him back. He spun around and grabbed the barrel of the gun in my right hand. We struggled for a moment. I had my finger on the trigger, and it went off." The bullet flashed with a crack out of the .38 Smith and Wesson revolver. It left the barrel of the gun at nearly 800 feet per second, burning a hole through the sleeve of Teece's red mack jacket, entering his wrist, and scorching a path up Teece's arm before passing out of his neck.

"I yelled at Teece, 'Are you hit? Are you hit?'" Honeybourn says. "I looked, and I had blood all over my hands."

Teece gasped and fell to the ground on his back.

Kajander, who had been climbing over the wall when the gun went off, felt the bullet whiz past him, but continued to chase the thieves who had already made it over the wall. He ran out to an empty street; there was no sign of the other three men from the car. "So I ran back and found Brian, who said, 'I shot him. I shot him!'" Kajander recalls. "He was very upset."

Teece lay semi-conscious on the ground. Battcock, muddy from slipping when he'd landed on the other side of the wall in the unsuccessful chase, heard Honeybourn shout, "For Chrissake, call an ambulance!" Although Mount Saint Joseph Hospital was just steps away at the end of the alley on Prince Edward Street, it did not have a twenty-four-hour emergency unit. As neighbours in their bed clothes began to come out to their balconies and peer from behind windows, they saw an ambulance appear just a few short minutes after Teece had been shot, which then rushed him to Vancouver General Hospital. Meanwhile, police backup units arrived on scene to begin a wide-area search for the men who had escaped. Kajander looked around the immediate area with his flashlight to see if a gun had been dropped. Both he and Battcock were certain they had heard not two shots, but three—the shot from Campbell, Honeybourn's shot during the struggle with Teece, and an initial gunshot, one they heard when they first stepped from the vehicle, loud and close enough that Kajander crouched down when he heard it. Blackburn and the other Clark Park gang members insist they did not have a gun with them that night, but Kajander still refuses to believe this. "I'm certain it wasn't a car backfiring, and to this day, I believe the guys in the car had a gun with them," he says.

Escaping from the alleyway and the police, Gary Blackburn hid in the shadow of a house. Alone in the darkness of some bushes for what seemed like hours, he tried to peer through them to see if the streets were clear, and wondered if Melo and Wadsworth had gotten away. "Every time I'd get up to leave, I'd hear a whistle or someone call 'Check over here,' but I couldn't see anything," he says. "Then it would get very quiet. It was spooky."

Blackburn saw flashlights coming toward the bushes, and then the light swing over his head. "The next thing I heard was, 'Don't move or I'll blow your head off.' They had a gun at my head," he says. As he looked up, Blackburn saw that the hands of the cop holding the gun were shaking. After they handcuffed and put him in the back of a patrol car, police questioned him about where he'd been earlier in the night, and if he'd been in the stolen car. "I told them I didn't know what they were talking about and that I'd passed out in the yard walking home from the Biltmore, but they kept wanting to know who I'd been with."

They drove Blackburn to the alley where the abandoned stolen Chevrolet still sat. Blackburn recalls there were fire trucks and ambulances everywhere. "With my handcuffs on, they pulled my arms up, which hurt like hell, as they pulled me out of the car. All these TV cameras caught me being taken out. I must have looked like a wild animal in pain like that. I know my parents later saw it on TV. It felt like the police were making a big show of it, like, 'Here we go, look at him, we caught him!' They took me down to the police station lock-up." At the jail, Blackburn half expected that he'd be interrogated or beaten. Unaware of what had happened to Teece, he nevertheless recognized that the mood at the station seemed more tense than usual.

Meanwhile, VPD Corporal Calvin Reynolds arrived on scene to escort constables Honeybourn and Campbell to Vancouver General Hospital where they stopped to check on Teece. "I saw the ambulance attendants walk out of the building shaking their heads. I knew then that Teece had died," Honeybourn recalls.

The men next headed to the Main Street police station where Reynolds took Honeybourn's and Campbell's guns for evidence—standard procedure in cases of officer-involved shootings. Reynolds noted that a single round had been fired from each revolver. Honeybourn was taken to the homicide department office on the third floor of the station, where he was interviewed by detectives Robert Desmarais and Sam Andrews. In a small room, he hand-wrote a witness statement and was questioned for forty-five minutes. Amongst colleagues, he believed he didn't need legal representation. "I didn't have a lawyer. I just told them the truth."

Gary Blackburn was also sitting in a small room. "When they put me in a cell, that's when they told me somebody had been shot," he says. "The first person I saw in the police station was Brian Honeybourn. He wouldn't look at me, he turned away. I knew Brian didn't like me—we used to deal with him when he was a beat cop in our neighbourhood. But I didn't know that he was one of the police who'd just been at the scene, and I didn't know what was going on."

Paul Melo was brought in next. Police had found him hiding under a car near the scene and brought him to the station. As he walked past Blackburn, Melo glanced at him, but said nothing. If Melo knew anything, he was keeping quiet.

"Then there was this beat cop we used to call 'Flashlight' who came by my cell," says Blackburn. "He carried a big mag flashlight, but he had it taped up so if he hit you with it, it wouldn't break. He came by my cell laughing, saying that one of us had been shot. He was trying to intimidate me, and said, 'Your friend's dead. Next time we're going to get you!' I thought they were playing games. So I swore at him and called him a liar and an asshole. I thought, *Why would he even say that?* And I told him to get the fuck away from me."

Blackburn got out of jail the next day and was not charged, though he believed that charges for the car and TV theft were pending. But at least he was free. His mother came to pick him up. "When I got in the car, I saw the look on her face. She told me that Danny had been shot and killed. It was all over the news. I screamed, thinking, *They finally got what they wished for.*"

ELEVEN: THE WRONG MAN

The morning after the shooting, the city awoke to news bulletins that an unnamed seventeen-year-old Vancouver youth had been shot and killed by Vancouver police after a three-hour-long police stakeout of a stolen car. While graveyard-shift news reporters monitoring police scanners had quickly arrived on the scene in the morning, more newspaper and radio reporters and TV camera operators flocked to the 300-block of East 14th to interview neighbours and take film footage. Police investigators were busy processing the scene for evidence. But before the media arrived in full force, Alexander Beaton, a forensic analyst and chemist with the VPD, found the bullet that had exited Teece's neck. It lay on the ground behind the Prince Edward Manor apartments below a blood-spattered dryer vent that it had hit before it fell to the ground.

The Sun

FINAL

PRICE 15 CENTS

Youth killed in police stakeout

LATE FLASHES

Shooting probed by city force

Guaranteed jobs urged

63 die as plane explodes

SEEKS JOB AT TREATMENT CENTRE

Harry wins health battle

Serious labor shortage hits B.C. forest industry

Trudeau to visit Heath

Danny Teece's death makes the headlines. SOURCE: *Vancouver Sun*

After giving his statement to supervisors, Brian Honeybourn left the station at five a.m., returned to his home in East Vancouver, and told his wife that they needed to pack their bags. They would head to the home of Honeybourn's parents in Delta, a thirty-minute drive outside Vancouver. VPD superintendent Tom Herdman had told Honeybourn that he and his wife should vacate their residence in the wake of the shooting.

The media attention was one concern, as reporters would soon discover who the VPD officer involved in the shooting was, and descend upon his home, though Honeybourn and the other three police officers were not immediately named to the press. Herdman's greater concern was that, since Teece was a member of the Clark Park gang, there might be a violent retaliation for his death. Herdman ordered round-the-clock surveillance at the Honeybourn residence over the coming days, and officers stationed there were to be on the lookout for any suspicious activity. However, upon learning about Teece's death, most of the gang were more stunned than immediately given to thoughts of revenge.

Oakalla Prison, 1975.
PHOTO: Dan Scott, *Vancouver Sun*

Mark Owens woke up in Oakalla prison that morning to hear the news that there'd been a shooting in East Vancouver. "We didn't know who it was, but word had gotten around that it was one of us [the Clark Park gang]." There were about fifteen Clark Park members in Oakalla then, along with a number of hangers-on. Owens recalls that that morning the prison guards removed him, Mouse Williamson, and others from their cells one by one and placed them on a single tier of the prison. Owens surmises that prison authorities hoped that, if news of Teece's death did provoke a riot, at least they could contain it to a single section of the jail. "Once they got us all together, they told us that it was Danny who had been shot and killed. I guess they wanted to let us all know at the same time before anyone else said something." Owens was shocked. Had it been Gerry Gavin, Wayne Angelucci, or one of the wilder men of the gang, it would still have been terrible news, but not as surprising. "Danny was a really laid-back guy. He was quiet. There were a lot of guys then who got into fights, but he wasn't one of them."

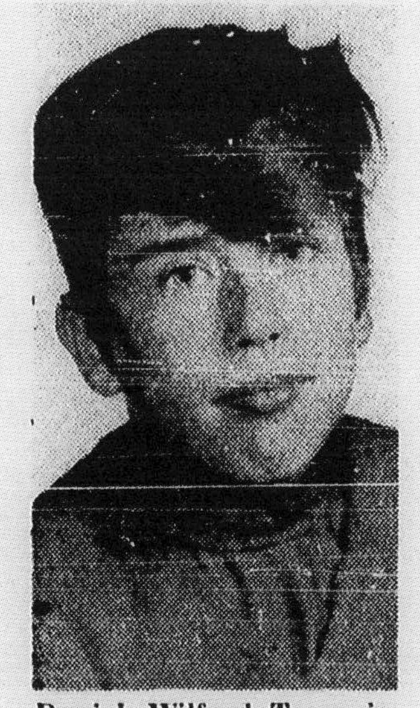
Daniel Wilfred Teece in his last school picture, taken two years ago.

Newspapers in 1972 ran the only available photo of Danny Teece, taken two years earlier when he was fifteen.
SOURCE: *Vancouver Sun*

Bradley Bennett was in the Salvation Army House of Concord, a correctional facility in Langley, BC, when he learned of Teece's death and was also shocked. Like Mac Ryan, Rick Stuart, and others in the Clark Park scene, he blamed Teece's death on the police "goon squad." "Everything that the goon squad had been doing culminated in Danny's death," says Bennett. "Danny Teece was a harmless kid. He had a bad gambling problem and was gullible. Wadsworth was the biggest criminal of the bunch because he'd been in and out of jail so many times. Danny had just come along for the ride."

Bennett believed that Teece's death was the result of the H-Squad finally making good on its threats; this was a widely held reaction in the East End. That Brian Honeybourn was not in the H-Squad and that the squad itself had disbanded a month earlier than the shooting were immaterial. Many East Vancouver residents, whether they were anti-police, sympathetic to Teece's family, or previously undecided, were now left to reconsider the message of the Clark Park Freedom Rally.

The next day, November 29, police named seventeen-year-old Daniel Wilfred Teece as the victim in the shooting. They revealed that two or three shots had been fired, but beyond naming Battcock, Campbell, Honeybourn, and Kajander as the officers on the scene, police did not specify which officers had fired and offered no further details.

Police were guarded in releasing information; this was, and is, typical protocol for an investigation that has not yet been concluded. To perhaps stem public concern that police had targeted Teece, Deputy Chief of Police Tom Stokes stated in the press conference that the incident appeared to be an accidental shooting. "It's not as bad as it may look now," Stokes said. "From the evidence, this was no case of drawing a bead on a man and pulling the trigger," and he declined to elaborate further on his statement, concluding that full details wouldn't be released until an inquest was held.[56]

After Stokes' press conference, newspapers ran the most recent available photo of Danny Teece—a school yearbook photo taken two years earlier when he was fifteen. Teece looked young to begin with, but his baby-faced looks at fifteen made him appear even younger. It was nearly unimaginable, in the public's perception, that such a boy could have been a criminal; he looked like any young teenager in a schoolyard on the way to class.

The day of the press conference, Arthur Teece, Danny's father, was interviewed for the CBC television news. Visibly shaken, he stated that he still hadn't been given the details of what had happened to his son. When the reporter inquired if Danny had ever been involved with violent crime, Teece replied that he had not seen his son in three weeks and confessed that Danny was no angel. "Stupidity," he explained. "Getting in trouble, stealing cars, breaking and entering." In a voice breaking with emotion, he stressed, "But not anything with violence ... I don't care if he robbed a bank, there was no need for this."[57]

In the initial days after the incident, the public knew less than Danny's father, and there was a sense that the police must have been completely at fault; details unknown, conjecture took over. With a Vancouver civic election scheduled for December 13, the subject of the shooting was raised during an all-candidates meeting at the Fraserview Community Centre, when Non-Partisan Association candidate Russell Fraser told those gathered—although he had no knowledge of the facts—that police had fired "all over the darned place." Fraser condemned the action, saying that, "They [the police] would have caught them eventually."[58]

That day, Robert Wadsworth also turned himself in to police in a dramatic

56 Stan Shillington, "Youth, 17, Fatally Wounded after Stakeout by Police," *Vancouver Sun*, November 29, 1972, 1.
57 Ibid.
58 "Candidate Criticizes Police in Shooting of Fleeing Youth," *Vancouver Sun*, November 29, 1972, 5.

fashion. He'd first done a taped interview, where he related the events of that evening to the *Vancouver Sun*, which would lead to a front-page news story. He stated that he had not heard a police warning, nor had officers identified themselves as police. Immediately after the interview, the *Sun* noted that Wadsworth was escorted to the Main Street police station.

Other media were not above exaggeration or incorrect reporting—especially the local alternative press. The most egregious example appeared in an issue of *The Grape*, which ran the inflammatory headline, "Was Danny Murdered?" The article went on to state: "Danny Teece, aged seventeen, is dead. But at this point there is precious little else about his death at the hands of Vancouver police that is clear ..." The author incorrectly reported that "Danny Teece was hit from behind on the left side of the neck." *The Grape* further noted that, "Today, the atmosphere in [Clark Park] is tense and sombre—and angry," quoting one unnamed Clark Park gang member as saying, "We ain't saints, but we sure ain't killers."[59] The unnamed source told the reporter that they had been involved in a variety of hassles with the police and the courts since the Rolling Stones concert, when a number of police had been injured. *The Grape*'s report did much to spread rumours in the East End that police had shot Teece in the back while he was running away, which many people wrongly believe to this day.

Meanwhile, temporarily taken off duty, Brian Honeybourn remained at his parents' house in Delta. "I was in shock and in a haze for a few days when my lawyer called me and said that we had to meet down at the police station," he says. Honeybourn's lawyer, Jack McGivern, and his police-union appointed counsel, George Murray, joined him there. Honeybourn returned to the homicide office where he'd previously made his official statement on the night of the shooting, and there he unexpectedly learned that he would be charged with criminal negligence causing death.

Initially, the case had been scheduled to go to a coroner's inquest, but on the night before the inquest, coroner Glen MacDonald received a telegram from new Attorney General Alex MacDonald (no relation) instructing him to call it off. Instead, a preliminary inquiry would take place to see if there was enough evidence to merit a trial. While it was standard procedure for the city prosecutor to take over and the inquest be suspended if criminal charges were filed during the coroner's proceedings, it was less common that the order to call

59 "Was Danny Murdered?" *The Grape*, November 29, 1972, 3.

off the inquest come directly from the attorney general's office. In addition, an inspector from the Ministry of Justice, Allan Nichols, was appointed to act as an observer during the inquiry, "to look at and attend the inquest on behalf of the attorney general."

It's uncertain if the attorney general's office took a direct interest in the case because the ministry believed that a coroner's inquest was insufficient, or if they felt that, in the broad interest of justice, the evidence should be given the priority of a judge's decision. Either way, it added a further tone of gravity to the case. No matter who had instigated the charges, if convicted, Brian Honeybourn would be fired from the police department and face prison time.

Constable Brian Honeybourn.
PHOTO: Courtesy of Brian Honeybourn

Honeybourn recalls that no one in the homicide department felt comfortable filing the charge. "This was back in the day when police laid charges instead of the Crown. When you filed a charge, you personally took an oath that you believed there were probable grounds for it," says Honeybourn. "But everybody in homicide had already learned about what had happened and thought I was innocent. So Lionel Smith, who was the head of the fraud division, filed it just to put an officer's name down for the paperwork."

Brian Honeybourn had joined the Vancouver Police Department in 1968, the same year as Esko Kajander and Paul Stanton. And like them, he'd wanted to be a police officer for as far back as he can remember. Honeybourn joined the police reserves in 1966 at the age of nineteen, and had spent rainy Friday and Saturday nights in a black police slicker directing downtown traffic at the intersection of Granville and Smithe streets. When he joined the department as a full constable at the age of twenty-one, he was assigned to the undercover drug squad. "This was when all the hippies were down on 4th Avenue. We were down there for a few months and had accumulated about thirty-eight arrests, which was a big number for those days. It was mostly heroin, marijuana, and LSD," Honeybourn recalls. When he went undercover as a heroin addict, the department organized a temporary tattoo of track marks on his arms so he could convincingly mingle with heroin dealers. Like all young police officers, he then did a year of regular uniformed patrol duty before he was posted to the District.

Honeybourn states that he had never previously encountered Danny Teece on his patrol beats or even recalled regular prior dealings with the Clark Park gang. But like any Vancouver police officer at the time, he was aware of them and the almost mythic standing they seemed to have achieved. "Every criminal in the East End claimed to be a Clark Parker at one time or another, it seemed. They weren't a gang of organized crime figures; they were punks and delinquents. But they did cause serious trouble, and there were a lot of complaints from residents and businesses in the neighbourhood. I remember a guy named Max Rosenthal who ran a five-and-dime store at Commercial Drive and 10th. One night they poured gasoline through his mailbox and tried to burn his store down."

With the announcement on December 1 that Honeybourn's gun had fired the shot that killed Teece and that he would be formally charged with criminal negligence causing death, the shooting was again the lead news story of the day. For Honeybourn himself, as overwhelming as the experience had already been, an even greater stress lay ahead as he prepared to defend his actions. He knew that it had been an accident that occurred while he was doing his job—but he needed to convince the court.

While criticism of police from *The Grape* and *The Georgia Straight* continued, many others expressed their support of Honeybourn; the Main Street police station received dozens of letters addressed to him. "I received a lot of mail from the public, a lot of letters of support. The public was very good to me," he says. Honeybourn was grateful for it, and kept the letters along with his police statements and materials that would proceed from the preliminary inquiry hearing. The letters, excerpts of which are published here for the first time, capture the opinions of many Vancouverites then, opinions that counter those expressed in *The Grape* or *Straight*.

A number of those who wrote to Honeybourn believed that the media had taken the word of a criminal over a policeman, citing Wadsworth's interview in the *Vancouver Sun*. One emotional writer stated that he had "thrown up" when he read that the newspaper believed Wadsworth, "a convicted felon, [and] furthermore an escapee from the bucket." He accused the *Sun* of "blow[ing] it up to sell papers and damn police officers."

Another man, who lived a block away from where the shooting had occurred, wrote: "We learn with sorrow of your charge. It seems strange that we hire you to protect us. To confront the irresponsible and subversive segment of our society in the middle of the night while we are secure in our beds: then we deliberate hours to criticize a decision necessarily made in seconds. We are confident that you will be exonerated and wish to commend you for your selfless service to us."

Other sympathetic letters expressed anger, and with Christmas approaching, many people opened their chequebooks. One woman, the manager of a downtown hotel, wrote, "Hope you don't let this experience spoil your Christmas. I have talked to many people. They all feel as we do. We would have done the same thing. I would have shot all four. We need more men like you. Please buy a little xmas [sic] cheer with enclosed cheque." "In a lot of the letters were cheques saying 'police under this kind of scrutiny and off work for doing their job shouldn't be allowed—go take yourself out for dinner,' and stuff like that," Honeybourn says. "The cheques I sent back, and my wife and my mother answered all the letters."

Some correspondence was sent directly to the police station addressed to Chief Constable John Fisk. Someone from Burnaby wrote: "A policeman's job is to protect the public and uphold the laws of our so-called society ... There is no question in my mind the problems with our present society are a direct and flagrant disregard of some of our younger generation towards the community and the policeman who represents such community."

In another letter sent to Chief Fisk, a senior living in the Marpole neighbourhood wrote: "As citizens of Vancouver for sixty years, my husband and I feel that the Police union (or whatever) should stand by their fine young men. You send them into a dirty job, dealing with 'punks' who are drunk or on drugs or goodness knows what else. Surely the policeman should have his gun cocked and ready to shoot wisely in an instant if the hooligans do not obey. Otherwise, when will we get law and order? If people (young or old) will tangle with the law, they must understand they must take the consequences (even being shot). We feel it is most unfair to publicize this 'disciplining' of Constable Honeybourn. It's only catering to open line sob sisters [i.e., talk-radio call-in shows]. Keep this stuff out of the papers. Ignore reporters and just try to keep law and order as you are appointed to do."

The preliminary hearings for *Regina vs. Brian Honeybourn* took place at Vancouver's Main Street courthouse. Today, in an officer-involved shooting causing death, a trial might not be heard for two or three years, but the preliminary inquiry began on December 13, 1972, barely two weeks after the shooting.

Instead of a local judge, it was determined that a judge from outside the city with no direct ties to the Vancouver police would be seen to have no personal bias in the case. Provincial Judge Eric Winch from Parksville, the senior magistrate for the district of Nanaimo on Vancouver Island, was selected for duty. Winch began the inquiry by reading the statutory warning to Honeybourn that he need say nothing in his defence at the hearing, but that if he did, anything he said would used in a higher court trial. Honeybourn replied, "I have nothing to say at this time, Your Honour."

City prosecutor Stewart McMorran would try the case for the Crown, and George Murray and Jack McGivern would act as lawyers for Honeybourn. While Honeybourn's statement was entered into evidence, the main testimony from the police would come from Esko Kajander, Ian Battcock, Bruce Campbell, and Corporal Calvin Reynolds. Much of the remaining testimony came from fifteen eyewitnesses, most of them residents of the immediate area surrounding the alley behind the Prince Edward Manor apartment building as well as staff from nearby Mount Saint Joseph Hospital. Among the witnesses was Richard Underwood, the second-storey tenant at the Prince Edward Manor who was awakened that night by the noise below his window. He revealed the remarkable coincidence that he knew Danny Teece from around Clark Park—not specifically from the gang but through friends who "knew people" around the area.

The theory that three shots had been fired instead of two was raised in the inquiry. Media critics of the police suggested that they had made up the story, which was designed to leave the impression that other guns were involved and thus police were justified in drawing their revolvers. Most of the eyewitnesses were reasonably sure they'd only heard two shots. Both Battcock and

Kajander insisted they'd heard three shots. The one witness who was certain she'd heard three shots was the furthest from the scene. Mrs Lily Pokrandt, who lived a street and an alleyway away, heard two shots in short succession and then a third. When McMorran cross-examined her, asking if she'd heard the sound of gunfire before that night, she assured the court that she had; Mrs Pokrandt had lived in Germany during World War II and stated she was acutely familiar with the sound.

While most of the attention in the lead-up to the hearing had focused on Brian Honeybourn, the inquiry delved into what was perhaps the real turning point of that night, the moment when Bruce Campbell drew his revolver. When Campbell slipped on the wet ground and accidentally fired his gun as he fell, he arguably set the tragic events in motion. During the first part of Campbell's testimony, he described in detail the earlier part of the night. But when questioning reached the point where the police cars boxed in the stolen Chevrolet and Campbell got out of the car, he stated: "As I got out, I drew my gun from my holster, which was a hip holster. At this time I heard—or I personally shouted, 'Police, stay where you are' ... I started to run west between the wall and the left front fender of the police vehicle ... As I was running, I slipped, lost my footing, and the gun discharged into the ground. The gun was pointed downwards at the time."

Prosecutor Stewart McMorran then asked what some considered the most important question of the hearing: "Could you tell His Honour what was the reason you drew your pistol or your revolver?"

"Well, I drew my revolver because at the time I felt it was a potentially dangerous situation," Campbell replied.

Honeybourn's lawyer George Murray cross-examined Campbell, asking for more detail. He noted that Campbell had been with the VPD for seven years and had considerable training. Campbell, in other words, was familiar with the proper police protocols for drawing a revolver. "Is there a situation that is described as a potentially dangerous situation, or a regulation governing that?" Murray asked him.

"There's no regulation specifically governing every situation," Campbell replied. "It is more or less left to the discretion of the individual constable involved."

Murray then dismissed the witness. Campbell might have thought there would be nothing further, but Judge Winch asked how Campbell's gun had been fired.

"I really don't know, Your Honour," Campbell said. "Here again, I can only assume that I had my finger inside the trigger guard. I know the gun was pointed downwards ... I can only assume that when I slipped, I tightened up, and the gun fired."

The defence made considerable effort to question the men who had stolen the vehicle. Wadsworth, Melo, and Blackburn were given the protection of the *Canada Evidence Act*, ensuring that they were free to describe how they had stolen the car and TV set without fear that they would be charged after testifying.

Defence lawyers will often advise their clients to wear a suit to courtroom hearings and appear as well-groomed as possible to avoid, at least superficially, looking like a guilty person. Robert "Bum" Wadsworth appeared on the witness stand in the same clothing that he wore when he had turned himself in: jeans and a red mack jacket. As an escapee from the Haney Correctional Institute at the time of the shooting, he personally was prison bound, and reasoned it wouldn't have mattered how businesslike or professional he dressed for the hearing. But the nature of his attire would come up in court. As George Murray grilled Wadsworth about several details, the lawyer took Danny Teece's red mack jacket, which had been entered into evidence, and held it up to Wadsworth. It was identical to the one Wadsworth wore. Murray asked him in a hectoring tone if the jacket was an identifying mark of the Clark Park gang. Wadsworth laughed.

"Are you finding something funny about this, witness?" Murray asked.

"Yeah, you," replied Wadsworth.

When the time finally came for Gary Blackburn to take the stand, he felt tense and uncomfortable as the lawyers went over the details of the night of the shooting. "I remember thinking over every question and if I should answer it. Even though they told me that what I said I'd done was under immunity by the *Canada Evidence Act*, I wondered: if I said something that the others had done, would they get charged? I was nervous."

For much of Blackburn's testimony, he kept his eyes on Brian Honeybourn, wanting to see his reactions. But as the questioning progressed, Blackburn realized that he was not there to testify about the tragic death of his friend, but about whether or not Honeybourn could be charged for it. "It felt like they were just trying to make us out to be the bad guys," he says.

At the end of Blackburn's testimony, Judge Winch asked him if there was anything else he wanted to say that was material to the case. Blackburn immediately thought of that night in jail after the shooting when the police officer nicknamed Flashlight had goaded and threatened him. "Well, just that the cops were laughing and saying 'your friend's dead,'" Blackburn replied.

"Well, that's unfortunate, perhaps," Winch said. "But what I'm concerned about is how the thing [the shooting] happened." Then Winch dismissed him from the stand.

Gary Blackburn left the courtroom quickly. He was angry that the court didn't want to know more about how Flashlight had acted and what he had said, taunting him about Teece's death. But Winch was correct; the court's duty was only to address the case at hand. "To me, sitting through the whole hearing felt like something just to make it look legitimate why they were able to shoot a seventeen-year-old boy," Blackburn says bitterly. "The whole thing seemed like a joke. They didn't ask us the right questions."

The hearing lasted a full day and a half. Supporters of Honeybourn considered the verdict just and expedited, but Danny Teece's family and friends in the East End felt the judge had given the evidence a cursory whitewash. Winch did not even need to recess the court to give his judgement. He began by thanking both teams of lawyers for allowing him to ask his own questions during the proceedings. Winch emphasized this was not a case in which the court had to "take one side or another side, but rather that we seek to find what is the truth and what occurred."[60]

Justice Winch found no credible evidence that police had failed to identify themselves that night and even suggested that Wadsworth had committed a misstatement to the court. He addressed Bruce Campbell's actions in first drawing his gun and laid some of the blame with him, stating, "There is the duty of every officer when he draws his gun to use that gun in a skillful and reasonable manner. It may well be that constable Campbell's actions are not criminal negligence per se, but in the circumstances it could be examined in that light."[61] But Campbell wasn't on trial; Winch moved on to discuss the defendant in the case.

60 *R. v. Brian Honeybourn*: Before Provincial Judge E.R. Winch: Reasons for Judgement. (Vancouver BC. December 14, 1972.)
61 Ibid.

Considering Honeybourn's actions on that dark night, Winch suggested that Teece had been the author of his own death by stealing the car and putting himself in a situation in which he would struggle with Honeybourn for the gun. Winch stated that Honeybourn had taken out his revolver only when he thought that Campbell had been shot. In the final words of his summation, Winch said: "Honeybourn was completely justified in doing everything he did.

'Tragic accident'

Officer clear in lad's death

City police Const. Brian Thomas Honeybourn, 26, was cleared Thursday of a criminal negligence charge laid after his service revolver went off and killed a 17-year-old youth during a struggle.

Provincial Judge Ernest Winch, brought from Nanaimo for the preliminary hearing, found that Honeybourn was completely justified in having his gun out of its holster. The youth, Daniel Wilfred Teece, grappled with the officer and the .38 calibre revolver discharged.

"There isn't a single scrap of evidence of wanton disregard for others," Judge Winch said. "Honeybourn was completely justified in doing everything he did. It is a tragedy that Teece lost his life, especially during the course of a useless, stupid crime. It is equally useless that a police officer should be put on trial for doing his duty."

Honeybourn was one of four officers who staked out a sto-

City police Const. Brian Honeybourn, centre, is surrounded by fellow officers after judge's decision freed him of charge.

Front-page coverage of the verdict.
SOURCE: *The Province*

It is a tragedy that Teece lost his life, especially during the course of a stupid, useless crime. It is equally useless that a police officer should be put on trial for doing his duty. The crown has not proven there exists a *prima facie* case against Constable Honeybourn and I, therefore, discharge him from this charge."[62]

With that, the court was adjourned. A number of Honeybourn's friends and supporters, including more than a dozen VPD officers in the courtroom gallery, stepped up to congratulate him and his lawyers. A *Province* photographer also approached; cameras had not been permitted in the courtroom, so a sheriff ushered the photographer out, but not before he got a shot that made the front page of the paper the next day, with the accompanying headline, "Officer Clear in Lad's Death."

Brian Honeybourn, however, was not jubilant, as he'd been responsible for a loss of life. But he was relieved that the court recognized that the shooting had been an accident and that he'd done nothing wrong.

62 Ibid.

When the ruling was announced, most news outlets and columnists responded favourably to the judgment. Radio personality Jack Webster interrupted his daily CKNW radio call-in show to announce "the good news that Constable Brian Honeybourn's case has been dismissed." *Vancouver Sun* columnist Jack Wasserman gave an even more supportive statement in his column, noting: "On the basis of the evidence at the preliminary hearing, a strong case can be made that Constable Brian Honeybourn was a brave man who, despite the appearance of a gun battle, drew his revolver and continued the chase in that dark area."[63]

Alternative papers such as *The Georgia Straight* and *The Grape* took a different approach. In the lead-up to the preliminary inquiry, *The Grape* had suggested that Teece had been "stalked, hunted, and gunned down by the Vancouver police."[64] And in a provocative article published after the hearing had concluded, *Grape* writer Peter Burton stated: "In the death of Danny Teece, the police investigated themselves, and their friendly prosecutor acted more like their defence counsel in his eagerness for the verdict."[65]

Burton admitted that he arrived late to the hearing, so his damning piece on the judge's decision, without having heard all the witnesses' testimony, left his reporting open to considerable criticism. However, many East Enders, no matter what evidence was presented or what the newspapers said of the case, found it difficult to believe that two Vancouver police officers had separately and accidentally discharged their weapons that night. Those around Clark Park, especially Danny's friends, did not believe the shooting had been an accident.

"They said it was 'a horrific accident,'" says Rick Stuart. "Two accidental shots in one night? Isn't that amazing? How did they come up with that? To this day, when I see cops beating the shit out of people or shooting somebody, I think, *These people don't learn their lessons.* This has been going on for years."

In many ways, neither the preliminary inquiry nor the ruling mattered to Danny's family and friends. They had already formed their opinions. After the charge was laid but before the hearing had taken place, Danny's family and

63 Jack Wasserman, "Column," Vancouver Sun, December 15, 1972, 23.
64 Rick Ducommun, "Was Danny Murdered?: I've Never Heard of Anybody Accidentally Killing Anything," *The Grape*, December 6,1972.
65 Peter Burton, "Surprise Verdict in Case of Cop Who Killed," *The Grape*, December 20, 1972, 2.

Friends and family of Danny Teece gathered at Mountain View Cemetery on December 5, 1972.
PHOTO: Courtesy of Wayne Angelucci

Bradley Bennett, Dennis Magnus, Lyle Rye, and Mark Owens visit Danny Teece's grave, 1973.
PHOTO: Courtesy of Bradley Bennett

friends had gathered to bury him at Mountain View Cemetery in Vancouver. The family had requested that the headstone read: "Danny Teece, Murdered at Age 17 by the Vancouver City Police." But the cemetery management refused to use that wording and asked them to change it to: "Danny Teece, Killed at Age 17 by the Vancouver City Police."

Three days after the verdict, Brian Honeybourn was back on duty. "There was no counselling in those days. No debriefing. It was, 'Get back to work.' The department was good to me, but that's what it was like," he says. For a few weeks, he stayed at a desk job before being sent out on patrol to rejoin partner Bruce Campbell. "I never asked Bruce why he took his gun out," says Honeybourn. "I can't ask him now [Campbell is deceased], and I wish I did. To this day, I don't know why he drew his revolver. I'd never have drawn my weapon had I not heard that first shot."

The reaction to the court ruling in the East End raised concerns about the threat of revenge from the Clark Park gang. "A girlfriend of one of the Clark Park gang members told her father that there was a plot to kill my wife," Honeybourn recalls. "Her father walked into the police station one day and told the story. A supervisor, staff sergeant Snowden, called me in and said, 'You've got to get out of your house again.' So they put a silent alarm on my house, and we stayed elsewhere for a bit while things cooled down."

Mouse Williamson was still in Oakalla where prison management let the Clark Parkers have a service for Teece. "There were certainly a few crazy guys in jail that might have done something if they'd been on the street," Williamson recalls. "There was tension around Clark Park," concurs Gary Blackburn. "There were a lot of angry people out there then, even a lot of angry parents, and others who weren't even from the park mouthing off that they were going to do something." But he believes they were "just saying it for the recognition."

During this time, police learned that an East End thug named Eddie Miller (name changed) had boasted that he was plotting to kill Honeybourn to avenge the death of Danny Teece. But, as one police source who cannot be named here said, "Miller was a big talker, and he wanted to make a name for himself, but it was [later] learned that there was truth to his plan." It was enough of a legitimate concern at the time to apparently bring two members of the H-Squad, who had been working on other assignments, back to their old

Protest posters like this one began to appear around East Vancouver in the wake of Judge Winch's decision in the preliminary inquiry. SOURCE: Courtesy of Wayne Angelucci

posting. The squad members surveilled Miller for a period of time, then paid a visit to his residence one night. They allegedly told Miller that "if Honeybourn so much as caught a cold from him, he'd be in trouble," then roughed him up before bidding him goodnight. Afterward, Miller left his life of crime behind and became a successful local car dealer.

For Gary Blackburn, the death threat that Flashlight, the police officer, uttered in jail the night of the shooting still hung over him like a black cloud. His mother feared that police would make good on it. She made arrangements to send her son to Latchford in northern Ontario, a town of just a few hundred people where she'd grown up and still had family. Blackburn would stay there for five months after the trial. "I didn't like the idea of being shipped off, but I understood. I got tired of it after a while—half the town is related to me one way or the other! So I came back."

One thought followed Blackburn from Vancouver to Ontario and back again and stays with him still: he can't forget the coin toss that decided whether he or Danny would take the back seat. "Had I won the toss, I would have been the last one over the wall that night instead of him," he says gravely. Blackburn knows that there were other factors that night that resulted in the tragic outcome. He knows that life does not come down to a single moment on its own. But he still can't help but think of that night, that moment. "The flip of that coin saved my life and killed Danny. I'm probably why Danny died."

There would be one final chapter in the shooting of Danny Teece. A year after his death, Danny's father and grandmother sued not only Brian Honeybourn, but Bruce Campbell, Ian Battcock, and Esko Kajander for damages. The Teece family's lawsuit was to cover not only the funeral costs for Danny, but also—under the *Family Compensation Act*—for special damages, as Danny was expected to be the provider for the family in future. Before the lawsuit was filed, in January of 1973, Arthur Teece, who was well-known to downtown beat constables for being drunk in public, broke his arm in an altercation during an arrest by VPD officers.

The incident with Arthur Teece deepened distrust of the police in the East End where members of the community who had been upset by the outcome of the criminal negligence charge supported the Teece family's lawsuit. Others criticized the family, saying they were motivated by financial gain. One caller to a local talk-radio news show accused the Teeces of estimating their son's future earning potential as comparable to that of a brain surgeon.

The Teeces' case was not heard until June 1974. George Murray would return to act as Brian Honeybourn's lawyer. The Teece family lawyer, John Laxton, argued aggressively that police had been irresponsible in drawing their revolvers, and their actions alone were responsible for Danny's death. Once again, the events of that fatal night made the daily local news.

And once again, the Teece family would leave the courtroom feeling justice had not been served. On July 23, 1974, the Supreme Court of British Columbia dismissed the charges against Campbell, Battcock, and Kajander altogether, as well as any claim for their son's future earnings. The court also ruled that Danny Teece had been eighty percent responsible for his own death; Brian Honeybourn had been twenty percent responsible. The ruling also allowed the Teece family to recover damages against Honeybourn as the sole defendant for twenty percent of Danny Teece's funeral costs. The amount was $48.00.

TWELVE: EAST VAN ELEGY

The death of Danny Teece signalled a change for the Clark Park gang, and some say the event marked the end of an era. "They murdered him. When Danny died, that's how the [gang] broke up," says Mac Ryan. "[We] would have broken up anyway, but Danny's death hastened it. It wasn't just that we weren't hanging in the park anymore and instead going to bars. We were all getting older then too, entering our early twenties. A lot of people drifted off, got married, got jobs, became *responsible adults*!" he says with a smile. "But Danny's death was a big deal. It was a pretty sad time."

For those who refused to believe that Teece's death had been an accident, the ongoing police harassment had evidently grown beyond roughing up the worst troublemakers on the street; it appeared that police were now ready to kill them. Others in the gang realized that what had happened to Teece might have happened to any one of them, on any given night. Each man had to decide how much he wanted to continue a wild life of fights and burglaries. "When Danny died, people watched their backs more," Ryan says. "I [tried to be] safer in things I did—it made me think twice. But [Danny's death also] made people more intense and meaner. It made me meaner for a time, I know."

Gary Blackburn, 2016.
PHOTO: Erik Iversen

After Teece's death, Gary Blackburn avoided further trouble. In 1975, he met his future wife and later went on to have three children. For a time, he worked at a fish-processing plant, and later he swung a hammer for Wayne Angelucci's family-run roofing business. Blackburn's wife passed away in November of 1998—the same month in which Danny was killed; with too many bad memories, he's felt low during that month every year. He has not remarried. "When you had something as good as I had, you don't fall into something again that easily," he says wistfully. But he's seen too much of life to give in to November's depression—he's already been through it all.

Now in his early sixties, Blackburn works as a personal trainer. Although recent open-heart surgeries have slowed him down a little, he remains active and is upbeat. Today, when he thinks back on his younger life, he can see how his own story is also woven into the history of East Vancouver. The park-gang era, especially the mythology of the Clark Park gang, still contributes to East Van's image as a bad-ass neighbourhood, and he takes some pride in that. But he isn't saying that the gang's criminal activities should be valourized. "I used to say, when I was younger, that we were going to create something, and good or bad, they are going to remember us!" Blackburn now says, laughing. He explains that it's the sense of solidarity that he and his friends helped to plant in East Van that is the important legacy.

"We changed the East End. At one time, everyone just looked out for themselves; everyone wanted to be king of the mountain. We brought all these guys who used to fight each other together to become friends. That created a family of people, hundreds of them, who stuck together. There was a real brotherhood that would go to the very end for you. It wasn't based on money but just that we stuck together. People would come from everywhere if you were in trouble. Even people who didn't know you had your back. People still say, 'Don't fuck with the East End.' All that East Van graffiti and what it means—that's because of us."

Police and other critics of the gang believe that their legacy is too stained with violence to be glamourized for its fraternal bonds. Many of the gang members are now not without regrets, but most believe that, however violent their youths, being in the gang strengthened their character and made them who they are today.

"Sure, there are things I wished had worked out differently," says Blackburn. "A lot of friends have died violently—alcoholism, drug addition, some were killed. I've lost as many friends as a soldier in war. There aren't many of us left today. The only time we get to see one another these days is at funerals or at East Van reunions." This annual invitation-only party is held at an east-side Legion hall. Old friends reunite to raise funds for charity over a night of

Brian Honeybourn, 2016.
PHOTO: Aaron Chapman

beer and some classic rock, with Vancouver's own Al Walker occasionally coming to perform. At the East Van reunions, the crowds get a little older every year, and most are now in their early sixties. To them, Danny Teece is forever seventeen years old. While there is a lot of laughter, jokes, drinking, and dancing at the reunions, tears are often shed for those no longer with them, and it's easy to imagine, even after all this time, that a few of those tears are for Teece.

He is still present in Gary Blackburn's mind. Blackburn has never before spoken publicly about the shooting. "It's something I kept bottled up for a long time. I still have bad feelings about it," he says. "I still hate Brian [Honeybourn] over it—I don't know if I should. I'm sure it affected him. That kind of thing affects your life forever unless you're a psychopath. And as much as I don't like him, I don't think he meant to do it ... Maybe everything was just headed to a climax, a disaster. Maybe it was inevitable."

Brian Honeybourn would go on to an exemplary career with the Vancouver police department. After serving for many years on patrol duties, he worked in internal affairs investigations and later joined the BC Unsolved Homicide Unit, a province-wide task force that was mandated to investigate the province's more than 600 unsolved murders and cold cases. In that capacity, he spearheaded the re-examination of one of Vancouver's most notorious unsolved murders, the "Babes in the Woods" case about the bodies of two children found in Stanley Park in the early 1950s. In 1999, he represented the department internationally when he was dispatched as part of an RCMP forensic team sent to assist NATO investigators in Kosovo with the grim task of the exhumation of mass graves there and making identifications.

In 2001, after thirty-two years with the police department, Honeybourn retired. "I missed the job like hell for the first five years, but I didn't dwell on it," he says. He also tried not to dwell on the events of November 27, 1972, though he's never forgotten the details of that evening. While there's no question that Teece's death stayed with him, he did his best to not be haunted by it—a task made a little easier after he unexpectedly received a note from Teece's sister Yvonne who said that she forgave him.

Honeybourn, who will be seventy in 2017, sometimes finds it hard to believe so much time has passed since he was a young constable in 1972. "I just was a kid then ... I'm sorry things worked out the way they did. I didn't intend for them to work out that way," he says.

There's no question that the police department works under considerably different policies, technologies, and training than it did in 1972. Plainclothes police in the early 1970s were required to purchase their own leather holster, then little more than "a wallet with a gun in it" as one retired officer described it. Today, the standard-issue holster has a lock-and-release mechanism. If a VPD constable takes out their gun at any time while on duty, whether they fire it or not, the constable is required to write a report to explain their reason for drawing the weapon. The accidental discharge of a weapon while on duty is regarded as a serious infraction. Even police training is different—they are taught now that a trigger finger is to be kept straight and out of the trigger guard and only put in when the officer is ready or required to shoot. This is clearly meant to prevent the accidental or unnecessary firing of a weapon. What hasn't changed is the responsibility given to the individual officer, who can still decide whether a situation warrants or requires them to pull out their gun.

"What was hard for me when I went back to patrol was that I wondered if I could ever draw my weapon again," says Honeybourn. "I was one of those guys that was reluctant to, I suppose. But I did it if I had to." He was offered neither mandatory nor optional police counselling after the incident; today, VPD officers involved in a shooting must undergo psychiatric assessment before they can return to duty.

The modern political climate around officer-involved shootings—especially those that involve minorities, as in a number of recent and controversial U.S. incidents—attract as much if not more media attention than the Teece shooting in 1972. But the most significant difference is how the investigations into shootings are managed. Today, a separate provincial agency, the Independent Investigations Office, handles the cases instead of leaving the police to investigate themselves. "Formed in 2012, the IIO operates under the umbrella of the BC Ministry of Justice and conducts investigations into officer-related incidents of death or serious harm in order to determine whether or not an officer may have committed an offence."[66] Even when it seems obvious that an officer acted appropriately and justly, IIO investigations can take months. More controversial cases, such as the 2007 shooting of Paul Boyd, a distraught man killed by Vancouver police, may take years.

Honeybourn is aware of how different the case might have been handled today; he knows that it might have ended his career. Had Honeybourn been terminated, Vancouver would have lost a good policeman, who despite the tragic accident in 1972, went on to serve his city honourably. Today, he is active organizing and hosting retired police reunion lunches that help to raise donations for charity, which are often attended by 100 or more retired police officers from a number of Lower Mainland police departments and RCMP detachments. Brian emcees the events, at which old friends and workmates come to see one another again and toast friends who are no longer around. The gatherings are not entirely different from the East Van Reunions. And although one group shows up in jean jackets and boots and the other wears sports coats and ties, it might be difficult to tell them apart.

There was one final chapter between the Clark Parkers and Brian Honeybourn. One night in 1993, when Honeybourn was on patrol in the Downtown Eastside, he overheard on the radio that a suspected drug dealer named Robert Wadsworth had been arrested. It was just over twenty years since Danny Teece had been shot, and Honeybourn once again drove down an alley in his patrol car to find, this time, a much older Clark Parker.

"I pulled up, and there were two young patrolmen who were checking him up out—they busted him for a little bit of heroin. He was looking pretty rough. So I went over to him and said, 'Hi Bob, do you remember me? It's Brian Honeybourn.'

"'Hi Brian,' he said.

"'Are you going to be ok?' I asked him.

"'Yeah, I'll be alright,' Wadsworth said.

66 Independent Investigations Office of BC, http://www.iiobc.ca

"I moved to walk away, and Wadsworth turned, saying, 'Hey Brian, I hope you had a good life.'

"I said, 'You too, Bob. There's a lot of water under the bridge.'"

Bradley Bennett, 2016.
PHOTO: Erik Iversen

Robert Wadsworth was one among many in the Clark Park set who found themselves getting deeper into serious drugs in the years after 1972. "Hash, weed, and booze had always been the thing with us," says Mac Ryan. "But by around 1975 or '76, the other shit started coming in."

"I first tried heroin when I was fifteen," says Bradley Bennett. "But by the time I was seventeen, I was using it more regularly." Heroin wasn't difficult to find in Vancouver, and East Enders didn't need to look far for it. While Gerry Gavin's mother Ruth had been one of the most well-known heroin dealers in East Van, she refused to sell to any of her son's friends. More often than not, Bennett went to known locations where dealers hung out, some of whom even operated brazenly out of restaurants on Granville Street in the mid-1970s.

"There was a diner right across the street from the Austin Hotel called the Chick and Bull Restaurant. There were dealers who were regulars there. Another restaurant seemed to be just a front. The owner sold heroin from behind the counter. You'd go in and ask for a 'super-deluxe chicken dinner' or something like that—this plate that wasn't on the menu but sounded like it was—and you'd get a cap of junk for it," says Bennett.

Bennett had been on probation from a halfway house when he began working at a downtown gas station. When he realized he wasn't making enough money to make his car and insurance payments and support his heroin habit, he started to supplement his income by "pumping gas"—robbing gas stations with two other accomplices from Clark Park. "It was really easy back then. I had the car, and we'd drive out to Burnaby or New Westminster to do the rounds. You could get about sixty dollars from each holdup. There would be three of us, so we'd split it three ways, and we'd do three a night. Sixty dollars was more than enough to keep you going. One night, I had to work at my job at the gas station when the other guys wanted me to drive them someplace. I told them I couldn't leave the station, so they just decided to rob me and save themselves a trip, and they just cut me in later."

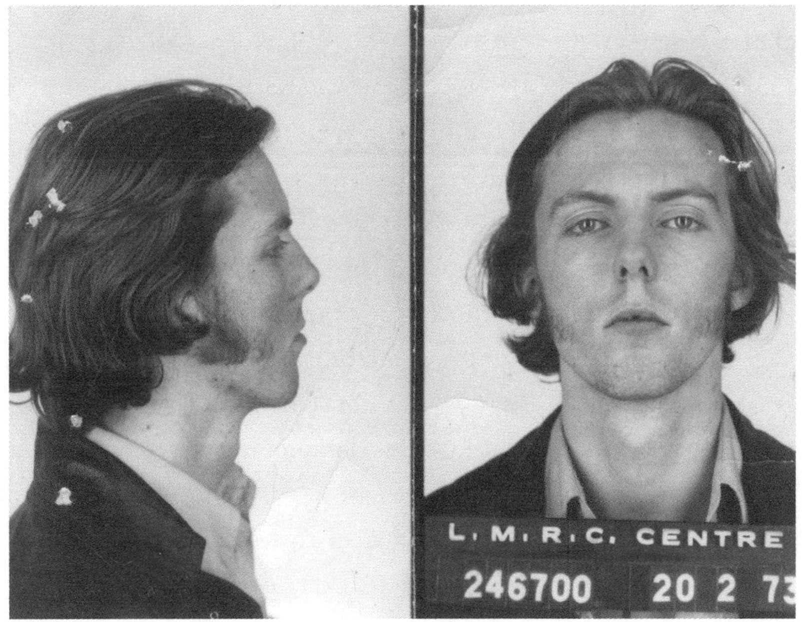

Bradley Bennett's Oakalla mug shot.
PHOTO: Courtesy of Bradley Bennett

Eventually Bennett and the others were caught and arrested, and he was sent back to jail. The sentence for the string of gas station robberies was two years less a day in the Haney Correctional Institute. Bennett recalls that it was an unpleasantly long separation from his new wife Irene, whom he'd married just before turning twenty-one. But Bennett had always been capable of capitalizing on circumstances—legally or illegally—and this time, he made the best of a bad situation. Haney Correctional maintained a full trade and technical school so inmates might learn a trade while they did their time. "You could take welding, auto-body, butchering, barbering, or automotive mechanics. You could pick whatever you wanted or, like Gerry Gavin, who was in there with me then, you could just push a broom and swing a mop. He had no interest in furthering his education or anything like that; he just wanted to do what he wanted to do."

On the recommendation of a teacher at Haney, Bennett signed up for a heavy-duty mechanics course. By the time he finished his sentence with a mechanics certificate, he was able to find well-paid work at heavy-industry job sites. Today, Bennett is surely the most well-travelled Clark Parker. The skills he learned in jail would take him all over Canada and even as far as Libya and Mongolia where he managed the maintenance of heavy equipment and diesel engines.

Noticing that many of his friends from the old neighbourhood hadn't survived to grow older, he also quit doing recreational drugs many years ago. Now aged sixty-two, he and Irene live in the south central interior of BC and recently celebrated their fortieth wedding anniversary. Like Gary Blackburn, he often remembers those of his Clark Park friends and acquaintances who were killed, overdosed, or simply died before their time.

"I always knew when I was doing something wrong. People who say, 'I was brought up in a broken home, I was abused, I never got any toys for Christmas'—fuck you. I made a conscious decision—am I going to steal it or not? Is that wrong? You're goddamn right it was, but I wanted it. I did it because I wanted money and I didn't want to work. At the time, it all seemed normal. I look back now, and [I see that] it was completely crazy," he says. "A lot of the stuff I did I'm not proud of. When you get older, your way of thinking changes. Back then, that's just what you did. We were just having a good time getting into trouble. You never thought about the consequences or the problems you were causing."

He's pleased about where his life has taken him, and it's evident that many of his old friends from Clark Park admire him for turning his life around and learning a useful trade that served him well when he got out. "Heavy-duty mechanics pays really well. I made more money working in that job than I ever did working as a crook—and it was a lot easier!"

By adulthood, Roger Daggitt developed into even more of a physical force than he'd been as a teenager. Years of dedicated weightlifting, both during stints in jail and on the outside, enabled him to break lifting and bench-

Described as the toughest man in East Vancouver, Wayne Angelucci "trained for the ["So You Think You Can Fight?"] event by running up and down the hill on 1st Avenue off Commercial Drive every day." PHOTO: John Denniston

press records in local gyms. Daggitt worked as a bouncer at the Biltmore Hotel pub and later became a professional wrestler under the name "Buddy Knox."

In the late 1970s, Daggitt showed up as a competitor in "So You Think You Can Fight?", a local boxing competition held at Vancouver's PNE Gardens, home to amateur boxing. The fights attracted a motley assortment of nightclub bouncers, loggers, bikers, and roustabout bruisers of varying fighting ability from East Vancouver to Williams Lake who travelled to compete for the $2,000 in prize money. Wayne Angelucci also entered into a competition in Vancouver, and Bradley Bennett participated in a match held in Kelowna, BC: "I didn't compete in Vancouver," Bennett says. "I didn't want to get matched up with [Daggitt and Angelucci]!"

Among the beer-bellied truckers and bad-tempered longshoremen who filled the ranks of the competition, Daggitt was known as a colourful competitor who liked to punch and head-butt lockers in the change room between bouts. In the ring, he employed a bit of the aggressive showmanship that would serve him well as a professional wrestler. His immense energy, whether it was an act meant to intimidate or part of his real personality, scared even seasoned fighters. Daggitt's evident rage would sometimes get the better of him, and he'd be beaten by more strategic boxers. However, he fought to the finals, losing against Gordy Racette, then a young boxer who would become a BC heavyweight legend. Racette later said, "I suppose that fight put me on the map ... as no one believed I could ever win [against Roger Daggitt]"[67] Later, Daggitt even squared off with his old VPD nemesis John Flaten from the H-Squad when both men competed in a local arm-wrestling tournament. But after Flaten insulted Daggitt, the ensuing war of words apparently broke out into a shoving match, and security guards had to separate the two giants.

Daggitt also continued his involvement in the Vancouver criminal underworld as "muscle" for Gerry Gavin. A new generation of police learned the name Roger Daggitt from a series of assaults and crimes for which he was arrested and jailed in the 1980s. "Roger sure didn't like jail that much," says Mouse Williamson, recalling a period when Daggitt was in Oakalla with him. "It wasn't so much the fact that he was being held in prison, it was because there wasn't enough food to eat, and he was still trying to maintain his protein intake and weight-lift as much as he could, even in jail."

In the 1980s, Daggitt became an enforcer and debt collector, acting as an independent operator who worked for anyone would pay him—including Hells Angels associates. One of these was a quick-tempered local stockbroker named Ray Ginetti, who'd been a financial advisor and money launderer for biker clients and for the Russian organized-crime figures who began to emerge in Vancouver at that time. Ginetti had been in a number of public fights (including one with actor Sean Penn) and had come to believe that he needed a bodyguard, so he hired Daggitt.

Police believe that when the Russian mafia apparently ripped off the Hells Angels in a $250,000 cocaine deal in May 1990, Ginetti's partnership with the Russians proved fatal. On May 9, 1990, Ginetti's wife opened a closet in their West Vancouver home to find her husband's body. He'd been shot once in the back of the head. A Cuban-American career criminal named Jose Raul Perez-Valdez was later convicted of the murder, but he

67 Gordy Racette, "The Story," http://www.gordyracette.com/the-story.html

claimed that Daggitt had hired him to do it. Daggitt never had to answer for the crime.[68]

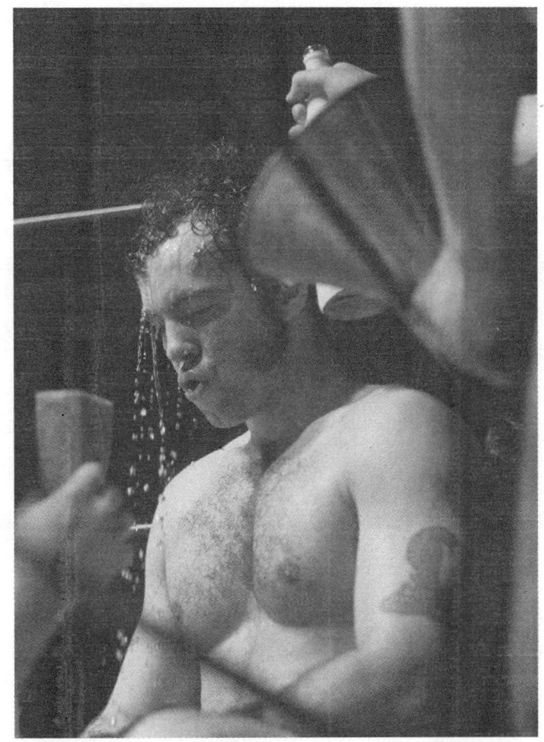

Wayne Angelucci c. 1970s.
PHOTO: John Denniston

In his day, he might have been one of the most feared Clark Park gang members and enforcers in the Vancouver underworld, but Daggitt came from an era of brass knuckles and bike chains. Now he was running with—and against—some serious organized-crime operators who did their enforcing with bullets. On October 6, 1992, Roger Daggitt, sat with his eighteen-year-old son over beers, watching strippers at the Turf Hotel, a run-down strip club in the suburb of Surrey. A man approached him from behind and shot him in the head three times before he fled the bar.

Daggitt's murder received considerable media attention. There was no mention that he'd started his criminal career in the Clark Park gang—the news reports said merely that he was "known to police." The RCMP, who were handling the investigation, told media that although the bar where he'd been murdered was busy at the time, witnesses were not immediately forthcoming with a description of the shooter. Some speculated that he'd been targeted because of his connection to Ginetti.

"I wasn't very surprised when it happened," says Bradley Bennett, who first heard about the shooting on the news. "Roger very likely killed some people himself. He never talked about what he did. He was always on his own and a loner like that. But everybody knew people hired him for certain things." "He got involved in some wild shit," agrees Gary Blackburn. "He

68 Neal Hall, *Hell to Pay: Hells Angels vs. The Million Dollar Rat* (Mississauga, ON: John Wiley & Sons Canada, 2011), 55–57.

forgot one of those things we all learned, which was always put your back to the wall."

Days after Daggitt was killed, a man from Montreal, Quebec, named Serge Robin was arrested for the murder. A professional hit man, Robin also killed a small-time cocaine dealer named Ronald Schofield and another street-level dealer named Ronald Pelletier.[69] While Robin pleaded guilty at his trial in the 1990s, he refused to say who had ordered Daggitt's murder. Robin remains in prison, and he still isn't talking.

Gerry Gavin continued on much the same trajectory he'd begun at Clark Park, getting drawn into more serious criminal activities as the years went by. "Gerry always swore that he would never do heroin, but he began to deal it on the side," says Mouse Williamson. "One time, I helped him cap up a bunch of it. I told him that he had better start sticking his arm to look like he was doing heroin. When you got caught back then with heroin, if you said you had it for your own use, you'd get a lesser charge than if you were just strictly selling it. But Gerry was hanging around with some rough people then and got pulled in deeper."

Vancouver police remained well-acquainted with Gavin into the 1980s. "Gerry was one of those leader-of-the-pack guys," says retired constable Al Robson. "He became a heroin trafficker just like his mother and a lieutenant to [local crime boss] Fats Robertson. Gavin was in Oakalla the same time as Robertson, and they met there."

"Gerry was kind of an extremist," recalls Gary Blackburn. "He'd go on some benders—drinking, blow, too much partying. We remained friends, but I saw less and less of him around then ... I think he had some enemies."

Maybe it would always have been difficult to imagine Gavin as a pensioner, sitting around at East Van reunions, reminiscing about old times. Many of his friends from around Clark Park had taken a step back as they got older, while he seemed to careen closer to the edge. "When Gerry died in the early 1990s, he was thirty-six," Williamson says. "Which is a shame. He had a son, Damon, who grew up to be a great kid. Gerry was in jail and off doing

69 Jerry Langton, *The Notorious Bacon Brothers: Inside Gang Warfare on Vancouver Streets* (Mississauga, ON: John Wiley & Sons Canada, 2013), 33–34.

his thing when Damon was growing up; he didn't really have him around as a father as often as he should have. Gerry never had his own father around. But Damon had a really great support system of other family and friends, and we all tried to keep an eye on him. Gerry would have been really proud of the way he turned out." "He wasn't always around, but I remember him being a good dad when I saw him," Damon Gavin says. "I have good memories of him. It was a sad time when he passed."

Other members of the Gavin clan have not been as fortunate as Damon. Gerry's twenty-one-year-old sister Lisa Marie Gavin was strangled to death in 1980. Her body was found in an alley in East Vancouver, and her death is believed to be connected to a group of killings known as the Alley Murders, which remain unsolved. But Gerry's mother outlived many of those who bought heroin from her, and she would also live to see the tragic deaths of her two children. Ruth Gavin died at age sixty-two in November 1993. Her death certificate stated that she had been a "Homemaker."

Rumours about the Clark Park gang continued for years after they'd essentially disbanded, and stories circulated throughout the 1980s and early 1990s about them showing up at house parties or storming local punk rock squats and stomping everyone in sight. The stories are difficult to verify. But if the Clark Park gang had indeed re-emerged in the 1980s, those who were described in those stories were young enough to have been the little brothers or sons of the original members. Perhaps a new generation of street hoodlums figured they could take the Clark Park name and reputation—but members of the original gang took issue. "We heard that there were these idiots who worked down at the PNE calling themselves the Clark Park gang," says Wayne Angelucci. "A bunch of us went down and straightened them out. They were really pathetic ... flashing their knives at people, bullying them. Just trash guys, and we sorted them out," he says without further elaboration. The Clark Park gang had a brand to protect.

The gang's look also endured as part of their legacy. The East Van cross, with which they'd tagged many buildings, would continue to be graffitied on walls all over the city, and their trademark red mack jackets would later be adopted by many local rock bands, from Joe Keithley of DOA to Bryan Adams and others.

After the death of Danny Teece, Mouse Williamson found himself in and out of jail for a few years, serving sentences for offences ranging from assault to running a marijuana grow-operation. Williamson spent more time in jail than others from the gang, and to survive he did his best to stay positive. "I was never ashamed to be a convict. Inside, I made the best of it so I wouldn't have to think about the outside world," he says. "He was a funny guy in jail," recalls Bradley Bennett. "He even had the jail guards calling him 'Mr Mouse.'"

Williamson and other members of the gang all served time in Oakalla prison; it was not unlike their days in juvenile detention in that a number of Clark Parkers filled the tiers of the jail. Some even started to recruit new members, and inmates from all over BC who had never even been to Clark Park were suddenly calling themselves Clark Parkers.

Williamson married and divorced and has six children and seven grandchildren. His eldest child, daughter Lana Williamson, admits that it wasn't always easy growing up in East Vancouver as the child of a well-known hell-raiser. "God knows I rebelled a bit myself, thinking I knew everything, but my father was always there for me," she says. Like many children of the original Clark Parkers, she grew up to distrust police. When Lana was about five or six years old, police came to the Williamson home to arrest her father on an outstanding warrant. "My dad asked me to get his cigarettes. I went to the kitchen table and ran back into the living room with them, and the cop said, 'He's not going to need those where he's going.' They just dragged him out of the house right in front of my face. He wasn't fighting them, and it wasn't necessary to do it that way. It seemed like they had no concern about what I saw or how I took it all in. I started to cry my eyes out. I knew he wasn't innocent, but all I saw was them being rough

Mac Ryan and Gerry Gavin at Trout Lake in the 1980s.
PHOTO: Courtesy of Mac Ryan

with my dad. It wasn't right to act that way in front of a child. They could have handled it completely differently. From that day forward, I didn't have much time for the police."

Today, Mouse Williamson lives more than 300 miles (500 km) away from Clark Park in the West Kootenay area of BC. His life is a little quieter in recent years. After his wife passed away, he considered moving back to Vancouver to be closer to some of his children and grandchildren. He has an air of dignity and charisma and a strength of character that many people who had less turbulent childhoods do not possess. He is very much at peace with himself.

"Would I do it all again? To be honest, ninety percent of me would. I suppose that ten percent of me—that everybody has—wishes that I'd done things a little differently. I was always an observer. I learned from the way I grew up and some of the situations I found myself in. Maybe if I'd been a millionaire running some corporation from behind a desk, I would never have learned those life lessons. I would have missed a lot of things. Even the bad times were valuable. No matter where I was in life, in jail or out, I was never ashamed of who I was."

Haney Correctional Institute in 1976. PHOTO: Dan Scott, *Vancouver Sun*

Williamson is proud of his accomplishments in later life, particularly after he took more of an interest in his Métis heritage. He has spent much of the last twenty years going to schools as a volunteer to teach kids how to create Métis-style carvings and talking sticks. He's also helped to organize a restorative justice program in cooperation with the city of Grand Forks in the Kootenays. "I suppose it's my way of giving back a bit," he says. "When we grew up, we were told that we were poor, from the wrong side of the tracks, and after a while you don't try to do better when you can. It took me a long time to figure that out."

Mac Ryan, 2016.
PHOTO: Erik Iversen

If the H-Squad didn't drive out the Clark Parkers, the rising cost of living in Vancouver certainly did. Rick Stuart and Wayne Angelucci still live in BC, but Mac Ryan is the only Clark Park gang member still living in East Vancouver. On a pleasant summer afternoon in 2016, he stops in Clark Park to sit on one of the park benches. As he looks around, the memories flood back. "I do feel bad for all the poor neighbours we must have driven crazy, raising hell out here," he says and laughs apologetically, then turns wistful. "I remember sitting right here forty years ago and saying to the others, 'Do you think any of us will live to see thirty?' Christ, not many of us did ... People got murdered, had car accidents, did drugs—there aren't many of us left."

Ryan continued his wild ways long after the Clark Park era. In the mid-1980s, he ran a profitable marijuana grow-op in a residential home in East Vancouver. One night as he walked home from a pub, he caught a whiff of marijuana. "It got stronger and stronger as I neared my house, and I thought to myself, *Man, somebody else must have a grow-op in this neighbourhood too, or they're having a hell of a party somewhere.* But as I turned the corner, I suddenly saw police all over my yard with flood lamps, pulling out all my plants, and I realized that the smell had come from my place!" Ryan fled the scene and crashed at a friend's house for a few days. One morning, his friend showed him the newspaper. It had Ryan's photo in a Crime Stoppers ad; he was one of "Vancouver's Most Wanted." Ryan turned himself in.

After spending time in jail throughout the 1980s and '90s, Ryan now leads a quieter life and works "here and there, staying out of trouble ... I used to joke around that I had a tattoo that said, 'Death Before Employment.' But I work every once and awhile digging ditches. I was at a job site once and a guy asked me, 'Do you know how to use a shovel?' I said, 'Yeah, I've hit a few people with one.' I made the foreman laugh, and they took a liking to me."

Rick Stuart (here in 2016) moved to Quesnel, BC, where for many years he worked as a first-aid attendant at a pulp mill. "Instead of shit-kicking people, I ended up as the guy who patched them up. It's pretty strange how life turns out." PHOTO: Erik Iversen

Ryan remains sentimental about his Clark Park days. Like many of the surviving Clark Parkers, he doesn't focus on the criminal activities they participated in as much as he remembers the friendships and camaraderie. Coming from poverty and troubled homes, they found a family of friends who supported each other when, in many cases, their own families weren't able to.

Ryan tries to visit Danny Teece's grave once a year. Last time, he bumped into the cemetery groundskeeper who told him there had been rumours that the Clark Park gang snuck into the cemetery at night and did drug deals there and that there were drugs stashed underneath Teece's tombstone. "I had to tell him it never happened."

"There's too many people here now," he says of East Van. "There's more coming. It doesn't feel like my town anymore. The city's gone now—it's changed so much."

The Clark Park Gang was *not* the last gang in town, but it was perhaps the last of its kind. By the mid-1970s, the park gangs had all but disbanded and were no longer a concern to police. Key gang members who didn't recognize the winds of change were like the dinosaurs before the comet hit. That comet was the rise of a new generation of Vancouver youth gangs.

As immigration patterns shifted, Vancouver became more multicultural and so did its crime problems. New Asian gangs such as the Lotus and Red Eagles, Latino gangs like Los Diablos, and Indo-Canadian gangs such as the Dosanjh brothers emerged in the 1990s. In Chinatown, traditional Asian gangs had focused on gambling, but the younger generation of Vietnamese youth gangs displayed a propensity for gun violence in public.

Danny "Mouse" Williamson, 2016.
PHOTO: Erik Iversen

Where the Clark Park gang members had prided themselves on their ability to fight, the new gangs preferred guns to bats, bike chains, or bare knuckles. Extortions and kidnappings superseded less profitable household burglaries or fisticuffs over street turf. Vancouver's new gangs were motivated by the considerable profits to be made in the international drug trade. Newer gangs, such as the Red Scorpions, the United Nations gang, and Independent Soldiers, have been involved in prominent murders, especially in the suburbs of Vancouver.

"We had a code back then," says Mouse Williamson. "We stuck together, but it wasn't money that brought us together like these new gangs of kids that have no brains, just killing each other over greed." The old-fashioned notions of gang solidarity and brotherhood that were taken seriously by the Clark Park gang weren't valued by the new gangs, for whom the park-gang era was as old fashioned as the zoot suit era had been to the Clark Parkers.

While many Clark Parkers grew out of the scene, got straight jobs, or moved

A reunion at Clark Park, 2016: Danny "Mouse" Williamson, Bradley Bennett, Rick Stewart, Gary Blackburn, Mack Ryan, and Wayne Angelucci. PHOTO: Erik Iversen

away, others continued their criminal exploits. Police believe that several graduated into membership of the Hells Angels, which officially established itself in Vancouver in 1983. However, many Clark Park gang members prefer not to say just who from their old ranks had joined the motorcycle gang. A strong respect for each other's privacy remains tantamount, as does discretion. While some Clark Parkers remain on friendly terms with the Hells Angels (they are, if nothing else, "old friends from the neighbourhood"), none of them advertise it.

There's barely a trace of 1970s Vancouver that still exists today. The city's downtown is now filled with residential towers of concrete and glass, and industrial districts such as Yaletown or False Creek are now also densely residential. The old decrepit homes of East Vancouver that had little value in the 1970s are now occupied by affluent owners; their refurbished character homes are spotlighted in city architectural history and heritage walking tours.

The Juvenile Detention Home was demolished in 1976. Both Oakalla prison and the District, the VPD substation in Oakridge, closed in the early 1990s and were replaced by new housing developments. Even the police have left their station, Vancouver's main police headquarters since the 1950s, at

312 Main Street. In late 2016, the city-owned building will re-open as an office building.

But it's not just the buildings that have changed in Vancouver. The generational divide that separated the law-and-order generation from the counterculture youth no longer exists. While a "smoke-in" turned into the Gastown riots in 1971, the annual 4/20 festival (marijuana rally) now attracts thousands of people. Where police once charged into the pot-smoking crowd with nightsticks, they now stand on the sidelines, smiling and shaking hands with festival-goers.

Clark Park is still there, in Vancouver's East End. But it's nearly impossible to picture it as a former haunt of a neighbourhood street gang. There's no late-night trouble in Clark Park these days. If you do enter the park late at night, you're more likely to encounter a dog walker than a threatening gang member. Although some say that Vancouver was better in the 1970s, the demise of the park gangs and the chaos they brought with them is one change for the better.

Mac Ryan, however, misses some of the grit that the neighbourhood used to have. As he leaves Clark Park in the late afternoon, neighbours with frolicking children enjoy sundown there. Ryan heads down Commercial Drive to Broadway, where he passes some young men wearing "Lords of Gastown" shirts made by a local clothing company whose name recalls the park gang era. Their trendy, '70s street-gang-inspired clothing line allows wearers to adopt gang fashions without paying the price of gang membership. Ryan keeps walking and doesn't notice them, and they have no idea that the older man they pass is the real thing.

A couple who look like they're on their way to a yoga class leave the Starbucks carrying a pair of designer coffees and hurry past Ryan. Just then, an early-'70s brown Chevy Impala heading southbound on Commercial slowly passes. It's a little rusted and not in mint condition, but as it heads up the street, you can hear the Rolling Stones "Rocks Off" from the 1972 *Exile on Main Street* album blasting from the car's open windows. Mac Ryan doesn't get a good look at the driver, but he smiles as the car drives past. Perhaps no matter how much the neighbourhood has changed, there are still a couple of greasers left in East Vancouver tonight.

PHOTO: Julian Fairfax Russell, 2016

AFTERWORD AND ACKNOWLEDGMENTS

It's said that history is written by the winners who make certain that only the most tourist-friendly version is remembered and represented—and for municipal histories, the winners are often found in boardrooms or on chambers of commerce. Thieves and policemen are rarely consulted, but they offer a unique perspective that other citizens are seldom privy to. We can learn more about our city's forgotten history and mythology by looking not only at its tycoons and traders, but also its cops and robbers. That's what I've presented here: history told by voices often unheard.

I must acknowledge many debts for this book. First to everyone at Arsenal Pulp Press: Brian Lam, Robert Ballentyne, Cynara Geissler, and especially editor Susan Safyan and production manager Oliver McPartlin who took to the task as if both the H-Squad and Clark Park gang themselves were hot on their trail, working under the once-again tight deadlines to finish. The text is immeasurably improved by their attentions.

The Last Gang in Town began in part when I wrote an article in the *Vancouver Courier* titled "Gangs of Vancouver" that detailed the history of some city gangs going back 100 years. It included a focus on the "park gang" era and connected it to issues of modern gang crime problems. The well-received piece came out when a number of shocking gang-related daytime shootings were taking place right in the city. For the first time since the era of the park gangs, Vancouver's citizens were thinking about the very public presence of gangs in their midst, and this led me to believe that a book on the untold history of this era would be of interest.

The publication of the *Courier* story eventually made it possible for me to meet some of the original Clark Park gang from the 1970s. Through in-person interviews, email, and phone calls over the course of much of 2015, I began to learn more of their stories. Interviews with former gang members and retired police revealed the fascinating thread of events from 1972 told in this book.

My thanks go to Wayne Angelucci, Gary Blackburn, Bradley Bennett,

Mark Owens, Mac Ryan, Rick Stuart, Robert Wadsworth, and Danny "Mouse" Williamson for telling me their stories. I am grateful for their time, trust, and candid discussions as I got to meet and know them over the course of the year. I have attempted neither to glamourize nor criticize the gang. They speak as participants from a different time and therefore a different city—and they speak only for themselves. They are not the only surviving Clark Park gang members—efforts to reach others were made—but it is remarkable, considering the lives they once led, that they are still alive to tell their stories when so many others are not.

Like every history writer in Vancouver, I give daily thanks for the City of Vancouver Archives and its peerless staff. I must also note my great thanks to Kristin Hardie, curator at the Vancouver Police Museum, who trawled the museum's photo collection to discover a number of surveillance and arrest photos—many never previously published—which coincidentally documented pivotal events in the Clark Park gang story, from the Rolling Stones riot to the Fraser Street party arrests. She had a hunch about several photos, and I was therefore able to discover that some of the same Clark Park gang members whom I'd been interviewing were captured by police flashbulbs more than forty years earlier.

My gratitude also goes to Sara Wotherspoon at the Vancouver Police Information and Privacy Unit for her diligence in tracking down the difficult-to-find, decades-old items I required. The photos of the investigation on the night of the Teece shooting are presented here for the first time.

My deep thanks and appreciation go to Sandra Boutilier and Carolyn Soltau at the Pacific Newspaper Group Library whose own detective work provided many images from the *Vancouver Sun* and *Province* throughout the book.

I am grateful to Jennifer Rosen who read and commented on the early draft, much to the advantage of the final text.

I am particularly fortunate in recent years to have been welcomed by a number of retired Vancouver police constables who have shared their stories—either on the record or off—as well as benefiting from their help with introductions and information, all of which have been invaluable. These encounters have been significant in helping me to understand the nature of policing in the 1970s and what an extraordinarily different world it was for the average police constable in a low-tech world. My thanks to retired constables Al Arsenault,

Vern Campbell, Wayne Cope, Chris Graham, Bill Harkema, Esko Kajander, Grant MacDonald, Al Robson, and Paul Stanton (name changed by request), as well as retired chief constables Bob Stewart and Jim Chu.

There are a few surviving members of the H-Squad, including one constable who was promoted as high as deputy chief, who all declined to be interviewed for this book. Unless those interviewed agreed to use their names (as in the case of retired constable Jim Maitland) or they are now deceased (as with Joe Cliffe and John Flaten), I have declined to publish their names. Some gang members preferred to have been left out of the story; surely the same consideration and respect should be afforded to those on the other side.

I must certainly express my gratitude to retired constable Brian Honeybourn for trusting me to tell his story about the remarkable night in 1972 when he suddenly went from being a young policeman on night shift to—in an instant—being thrust under the glaring scrutiny of the news media. This is the first time he has spoken publicly in detail about the Teece shooting. During the course of our interviews, he was candid, honest, and respectful. While the shooting was an undeniably significant incident, I learned that Brian Honeybourn was involved in many newsworthy events during a long and remarkable police career.

Honeybourn also entrusted me with his personal archive of court and police documents, court transcripts, witness subpoenas, newspaper articles, and personal correspondence during the investigation and preliminary inquiry into the death of Danny Teece, all which he has kept for more than four decades. It would have been difficult for me to have accurately told the story without access to official original documents. With the publication of this book, as per his request, those documents will be donated to the Vancouver Police Museum and will be available for public review.

Lastly, I must thank a number of others for various leads, helpful advice, and support: John Atkin, Squire Barnes, the Belshaw Gang, Rebecca Blissett, Gyles Brandreth, Mike Culpepper, Tracey Davis, John Denniston, Danny Filippone, constable Randy Fincham, Damon Gavin, the Honourable Judge Thomas Gove, Fred Herzog and Sophie Brodovitch at the Equinox Gallery, constable Toby Hinton, Rich Hope, Ken Johns, Verdon Jotie at Vancouver Provincial Court, Michael Kluckner, Jak King, Grant Lawrence, John Mackie, Laurie Mercer, Glen Mofford, Malcolm Parry, RCMP constable Franco Pirritano, Vince Ricci, Red Robinson, Erika Rodela, Rebecca Russell, Lani Russwurm and his Past Tense blog, Jason Vanderhill, Vaughn Worden, Lana Williamson, the Rolling Stones, the Clash, and everyone at Live Nation Concerts and the *Vancouver Courier*.

Today, Vancouver very much prides itself on its natural beauty and aims to become the greenest, cleanest city in North America—concepts far from the minds of those who lived in Vancouver in the early 1970s. Vancouver was grittier then—not the tragic grit still seen in the Downtown Eastside, but a tough, industrial, blue-collar grit that spread from Clark Park to Dunbar. Vancouver then had its Mean Streets. The reader may decide for themselves if Vancouver is now better off without them.

REFERENCES

BOOKS AND ARTICLES

"4 Policemen Hurt in Gang Attacks by Young Hoodlums." *Vancouver Sun*, February 25, 1963.

"7 Arrested on Drug Conspiracy Charges." *The Province*, June 24, 1972.

"A Real Estate Dodge." *Montreal Gazette*, June 27, 1907.

Arnason, Al. "Shot Kills Youth." *The Province*, November 29, 1972.

Bachop, Bill, and Honeyman, Scott. "Police battle mob at Stones' concert as firebombs, rocks, bottles hurled." *Vancouver Sun*, June 5, 1972.

Barnholden, Michael. *Reading the Riot Act: A Brief History of Riots in Vancouver*. Vancouver: Anvil Press, 2005.

"BC Delinquent Girls Housed in Damp Cells." *Calgary Herald*, November 11, 1954.

"Blue Meanies." *Georgia Straight*, June 22, 1972.

Burton, Peter. "Surprise Verdict in Case of Cop who Killed." *The Grape*, December 20, 1972.

Campbell, Larry, Dominque Clément, and Gregory Keale. *Debating Dissent: Canada and the Sixties*. Toronto: University of Toronto Press, 2012.

"Candidate Criticizes Police in Shooting of Fleeing Youth." *Vancouver Sun*, November 29, 1972.

"Clark Park Talk." *Georgia Straight*, August 3, 1972.

Chapman, Aaron. "Gangs of Vancouver." *Vancouver Courier*, February 4, 2011.

Craig, Jamie. "Stoned Young Bask in Music of the Stones." *Vancouver Sun*, June 4, 1972.

Davis, Chuck, ed. *The History of Metropolitan Vancouver*. Madeira Park, BC: Harbour Publishing, 2011.

"Dead Boy's Father Suing 4 Policemen." *The Province*, June 25, 1974.

Ducommun, Rick. "Was Danny Murdered?: I've Never Heard of Anybody Accidentally Killing Anything." *The Grape*, December 6, 1972.

"East End Feedback for the Ghost Squad Gang." *Georgia Straight*, July 20, 1972.

Fairley, Jim. "Police Testify They Heard Shot: Youth Died in Struggle" *The Province*, July 27, 1974.

———. "Heard Shot, Saw Officer Slump." *The Province*, June 26, 1974.

Ferry, Jon. "Officer Remanded in Shooting." *Vancouver Sun*, December 2, 1972.

Finlay, Michael. "Shooting under Examination." *Vancouver Sun*, November 30, 1972.

Foster, Leslie T., and Brian Wharf, eds. *People, Politics, and Child Welfare in British Columbia*. Vancouver: UBC Press, 2007.

Fotheringham, Alan. ("Column"). *Vancouver Sun*, June 5, 1972.

"Gangs, Glue, and Mao." *The Province*, July 22, 1972.

"Grand Jury Finds Conditions in Boys Industrial Home Appalling." *Vancouver Daily World*, December 13, 1918.

"Hearing delayed on brutality complaint." *The Province*, February 10, 1973.

Hertzler, Robert. "Vancouver's Juvenile Gangs 'Wiped Out' in Two Years." *Spokane Daily Chronicle*, March 17, 1952.

"Hoodlum Problem in Parks." *Vancouver Sun*, June 15, 1965.

"Judge Hears Different Accounts During Shooting Hearing." *Vancouver Sun*, December 14, 1972.

King, Jak. *The Drive: A History to 1956*. Vancouver: The Drive Press, 2011.

Kluckner, Michael. *Vancouver Remembered*. North Vancouver: Whitecap Books, 2006.

———. *Vancouver: Between the Streets*. Vancouver: Consolidated Merriment Ltd, 1981.

Langmann, Kurt. "You Sense a Riot is Brewing? Know When It's Time to Leave." *Aldergrove Star*, June 23, 2011.

Marshall, Roger, and Ed Simons. "Policeman Charged in Gun Death: Negligence Allegation." *The Province*, November 30, 1972.

MacDonald, Bruce. *Vancouver: A Visual History*. Vancouver: Talonbooks, 1993.

Middleton, Greg. "Gangland Heavy Executed at Bar." *The Province*, October 8, 1992.

McCardell, Mike. "Stokes Recalls Days of Street Justice." *The Province*, October 7, 1975.

McCormick, Christy. "Clark Park Harassment: Peaceful Rally Raps Police Action." *Vancouver Sun*, July 17, 1972.

McDermott, Ross. "Kosovo Experience Strikes Home for Local Man." *Peachland Signal*, September 21, 2000.

McGrath, Rick. "Rock and Roll Rip Off." *Georgia Straight*, November 25, 1971.

Morely, Alan. "Perennial Succession of East End Gangs." *Vancouver News-Herald*, August 2, 1944.

"Officer Clear in Lad's Death." *The Province*, December 15, 1972.

Outston, Rick. "It's a 'Frightening Name' But Police Can Cite No Links." *Vancouver Sun*, October 29, 1983.

"Pinkos—Vancouver Mayor Raps Opposition to Bridge." *Ottawa Citizen*, February 9, 1972.

"Police Testify in Youth's Death." *Vancouver Sun*, December 13, 1972.

"Policemen Injured by Street Rowdies." *The Province*, September 18, 1972.

"Policemen Attacked on Street." *Vancouver Sun*, October 20, 1972.

"Policewomen Saved from Teen-Age Mob." *The Province*, July 9, 1962.

"Punk Gangs Take Over English Bay." *The Province*, July 16, 1970.

"Rampaging Coliseum Crowd Sends Rock Stars Fleeing." *Vancouver Sun*, November 21, 1972.

Russwurm, Lani. "Street Fighting Man." *Past Tense Vancouver Histories*, November 12, 2009. https://pasttensevancouver.wordpress.com/tag/clark-park-gang/

———. "Early Vancouver Youth Gangs." *Past Tense Vancouver Histories*, July 27, 2016.

Shillington, Stan. "Youth, 17, Fatally Wounded after Stakeout by Police." *Vancouver Sun*, November 29, 1972.

Schnob, Rod. "Dear Mother, Dear Mother." *The Incarcerated Inkwell.* http://theincarceratedinkwell.ca/

Smedman, Lisa. *Immigrants: Stories of Vancouver's People*. Vancouver: The Vancouver Courier, 2009.

Spears, James. "Age Breaking Up That Old Gang." *The Province*, July 27, 1974.

Steele, Richard (Mike). *The First 100 Years: An Illustrated Celebration*. Vancouver, Vancouver Board of Parks and Recreation, 1988.

Swan, Joe. *A Century of Service: The Vancouver Police, 1886–1986*. Vancouver: The Vancouver Police Historical Society and Centennial Museum, 1986.

"Tall Tale by Police Alleged." *The Province*, June 28, 1974.

Taylor, Keith. "Young People Complain: The Police Discriminate Against Us." *Vancouver Sun*, October 5, 1972.

"Vicious Hoodlums Rob, Wreck House." *The Province*, February 2, 1952.

"Was Danny Murdered?" *The Grape*, November 29, 1972.

Wasserman, Jack. "Column." *Vancouver Sun*, December 15, 1972.

Wilson, Stevie, "You Should Know: The History of the City's Grandview-Woodland Neighbourhood." *Scout Magazine*, May 23, 2013. http://scoutmagazine.ca/2013/05/23/you-should-know-the-history-of-the-citys-grandview-woodland-neighbourhood/

"Youth Died 'Because of Own Recklessness.'" *The Province*, June 28, 1974.

"Youths in Vancouver Protest Festival Ban." *Montreal Gazette*, July 16, 1970.

Young, Mary-Lynn. "Police Fear Slayings Linked." *Vancouver Sun*, October 8, 1992.

———. "Montrealer Slain at Pub in Gastown." October 9, 1992.

TELEVISION

News, Vancouver. CBC Television. 3:10 Broadcast July 27, 1972.

Evening News, Vancouver. CBC Television. 1:18. Broadcast November 21, 1971.

Evening News, Vancouver. CBC Television. 1:55. Broadcast June 5, 1972.

UNPUBLISHED DOCUMENTS

Arthur Teece and Alida Teece vs Brian Honeybourn, Bruce Campbell, Esko Kajander and Ian Battcock. Examination for Discovery. Supreme Court of BC No. 25643, April 16, 1974.

Honeybourn, Brian, personal correspondence, December 1972.

Regina vs. Brian Honeybourn."Reasons for Judgement and Preliminary Inquiry Transcripts before Justice E.R. Winch. Vancouver, BC: December 14, 1972.

Vancouver Police Department. Detective Division. To S/Sgt. Devries, Drug Squad. Re: Clark Park Gang. Superintendent Ted Oliver, File Project H. June 13, 1972.

Vancouver Police Department. Report to City Prosecutor. Case No. 72-64202. December 5, 1972. Criminal Negligence Charge. Report by Det. D. Desmarais.

Young, Michael G. *History of Vancouver Youth Gangs.* M.A. thesis, Simon Fraser University thesis, 1993.

INTERVIEWS

Angelucci, Wayne. Telephone interview with author, March 22, 2016.

Armstrong, John. Telephone interview with author, June 5, 2016.

Bennett, Bradley. Interview with author, Vancouver, BC, November 28, 2015 and March 20, 2016.

Campbell, Ret. Constable Vern. Interview with author, 2010.

Galgoczy, Destry. Interview with author, April 26, 2016.

Galgoczy, Louis. Interview with author, April 26, 2016.

Blackburn, Gary. Interview with author, January 13, 2016.

Gavin, Damon. Telephone interview with author, February 28, 2016.

Graham, Ret. Constable Chris. Telephone interview with author, August 12, 2015.

Honeybourn, Ret. Constable Brian. Interview with author, Langley, BC, August 20, 2015.

Gove, Honourable Judge Thomas. Interview with author, Vancouver BC, February 25, 2016.

Jones, Nicholas. Telephone interview with author, June 7, 2016.

Kajander, Ret. Constable Esko. Interview with author, Coquitlam, BC, December 1, 2015.

Kruz, Jerry. Interview with author, March 18, 2016.

Maitland, Ret. Constable James. Interview with author, December 30, 2015.

MacDonald, Rod. Telephone interview with author, 2010.

MacDonald, Ret. Constable Grant. Interview with author, July 28, 2015.

MacNichol, Doug. Telephone interview with author, June 11, 2016.

Owens, Mark. Telephone interview with author, December 14, 2015.

Sharma, Vic. Interview with author, Vancouver, BC, May 16, 2016.

Singer, Keith. Interview with author, Vancouver, BC, July 18, 2015.

Stanton, Ret. Constable Paul. Telephone interview with author, January 13, 2016.

Stewart, Ret. Chief Constable Robert. Interview with author, January 16, 2015.

Stuart, Rick. Telephone interview with author, March 18, 2016.

Robson, Ret. Constable Al. Telephone interview with author, August 8, 2015.

Ryan, Mac. Interview with author, July 18, 2015 and July 28, 2016.

Wadsworth, Robert. Interview with author, Vancouver, BC, December 19, 2015.

Walker, Al. Interview with author, Vancouver, BC, May 3, 2016.

Williams, Danny "Mouse." Telephone interviews with author, October 28 and 30, 2015.

NAME INDEX

PHOTO: Rebecca Blissett

AARON CHAPMAN is a writer, historian, and musician. Born and raised in Vancouver, he has been a contributor to the *Vancouver Courier*, the *Georgia Straight*, and CBC radio. He is the author of *Liquor, Lust, and the Law: The Story of Vancouver's Legendary Penthouse Nightclub* and *Live at the Commodore: The Story of Vancouver's Historic Commodore Ballroom*, which won the Bill Duthie Booksellers' Choice Award (BC Book Prizes) in 2015. A graduate of the University of British Columbia, he is a member of Heritage Vancouver, the Canadian Historical Association, and the Point Roberts Historical Society. www.aaronchapman.net